Gobelin Stitch Embroidery

Gobelin Stitch Embroidery

Pauline Chatterton

CHARLES SCRIBNER'S SONS / NEW YORK

Library of Congress Cataloging in Publication Data
Chatterton, Pauline.
    Gobelin stitch embroidery.
    1. Canvas embroidery—Patterns. I. Title.
TT778.C3C46   746.4'4   78-11698
ISBN 0-684-16044-7

1 3 5 7 9 11 13 15 17 19   F/C   20 18 16 14 12 10 8 6 4 2

Printed in the United States of America

CONTENTS

ACKNOWLEDGMENTS

My thanks to Peter Maurer for his photography, Bucilla Needlecraft for providing the yarns, my editor, Miss Elinor Parker, Joan and Richard Chatterton, and all the others who helped in various ways while I was working on this book.

All photographs were by Peter Maurer, unless otherwise acknowledged. All yarn was provided courtesy of Bucilla Needlecraft in the following quality: Persian Needlepoint and Crewel Wool.

INTRODUCTION

It is the intention of this book to present a very simple needlepoint stitch, which is easily learned and applied, and to interpret a wide range of designs in terms of that stitch. In this way, rich design sources become accessible to a larger number of would-be needlewomen. The upright Gobelin stitch, which is used throughout the book, is simple to master, and because it can be worked over two, four, or even six holes of the canvas, the designs are quick as well as easy to make. Many people have the same fear of the blank canvas as the writer experiences when faced with the blank sheet of paper. However, the opportunities for creative adventure are far greater on a blank canvas than on one previously printed for you. The designs in this book are all counted work, and if there is one fear greater than that of an empty canvas, it is, perhaps, fear of following a chart. It is my intention to show the reader just how enjoyable, quick, and easy counted work can be.

The first three chapters describe the basic techniques required to work and complete all the projects given in the remaining part of the book. I suggest that you review those chapters briefly, even if you are thoroughly familiar with the stitches used and have previously worked a number of projects in upright Gobelin or Bargello stitches.

1

Many of the designs are given in the form of simple squares, which you can use as they are to make bags, pictures, or pillows, or combine with other designs and plain squares to create your own individual rugs and wall hangings. The squares should be treated like building blocks from which you can create designs to satisfy your personal requirements. This gives the greatest possible flexibility to the usefulness of the designs. You will not be confined to using one project simply as a pillow, but, with the help of the advice given in Chapters 2 and 3, you can branch out on your own to create an entirely new project.

I hope you will be inspired by the variety of designs provided to experiment as well as to work projects from the book. Charted canvas work, using very simple and quick stitches, can be fun and amazingly versatile.

materials
and stitches

The stitches used in this book are so simple that "even a child could do them." In my experience children frequently enjoy counted work, in simple stitches that cover the canvas quickly, even more than their elders. They do not seem to have developed a prejudice against counting and see a chart rather in terms of an amusing jigsaw puzzle, in which they fit the pieces together by sewing them on the canvas. Once the basic stitches are mastered, the designs can be as much fun for an adult as the jigsaw is for a child. This chapter tells you all you need to know about the materials you require, and the stitches to be learned, in order to work the projects that appear later in the book.

materials

Canvas Mono canvas is used for all counted work. The term *mono* refers to the fact that the canvas is woven with a single thread instead of the two used in Penelope canvas. Photograph 1 shows the single-thread weave to be found on all mono canvas. This type of canvas is always preferred for counted work, because one can easily separate the spaces between the threads, or holes, from the woven threads themselves. This is not always easy to distinguish on a Penelope or double-weave canvas, where the space between the two woven threads can create confusion when counting. With fewer vertical and horizontal threads to be accommodated, it is also possible to achieve finer weaves with single-thread canvas, an effect that is most desirable in straight stitch work.

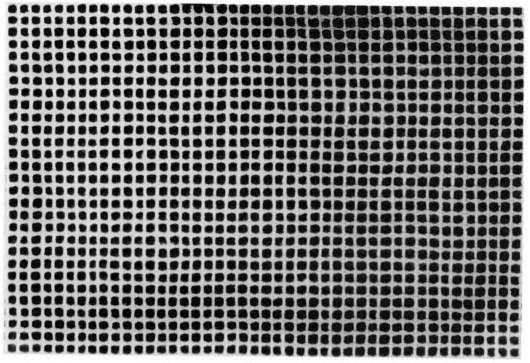

Photograph 1.
Mono canvas

Until recent years mono canvas had one severe disadvantage when compared with the double weave of a Penelope canvas: mono canvas was not nearly as firm. Stitches pulled too tightly during work could distort the canvas and lead to unsightly gaps appearing between rows of stitches. A new canvas has been developed that combines the single-thread appearance of the regular mono canvas with the firmness of a Penelope weave. This new canvas is variously called "interlock" or "leno weave." At each crossover point between vertical and horizontal threads of the canvas, the cotton is interwoven to create a firm "lock," which prevents the vertical and horizontal threads from slipping away from each other, even under considerable pressure. As a result of this feature in the weaving, leno canvas cannot unravel or fray in the way that simply woven mono canvases do. I would strongly recommend leno canvas to the beginner. I have watched many beginners become disheartened when working with regular mono canvas. We all have a tendency to pull stitches too tightly when we first start sewing. It is a great help to have a canvas to work on that will not distort, even under pressure, rather than one where the least heavy-handedness produces disastrous results.

Many experienced needlewomen dislike leno canvas because the additional weaving involved at the interlocking joins between vertical and horizontal threads creates a much stiffer canvas than the regular weave. One certainly cannot argue with this point. I suggest that the beginner, after finishing a few projects on the leno canvas, purchase a small piece of regular mono canvas and experiment for herself, to find which canvas best suits the projects she has in mind and her own capabilities as a needlewoman. Most people who I have taught, and who began sewing on leno canvas, object strongly to using the regular weave afterward.

Mono canvas is available in many different sizes, ranging from as large as seven to as small as twenty-four holes or meshes to the inch. I have chosen to use ten-mesh-to-one-inch canvas for most of the projects in this book, since it is readily available in regular and leno canvas. I have also provided some projects for work on eighteen-mesh-to-one-inch canvas for those who like finer work with more detail. The rugs mentioned in Chapter 2 should be worked on seven-mesh-to-one-inch canvas to achieve proper coverage with standard rug yarn.

Whichever canvas you are using, it is a wise step to bind the raw edges with masking tape before beginning to work. You will require tape of not less than 1 inch in width. Cut a piece of tape the length of the side of canvas to be bound. Place the tape, sticky side up, on your work table. Lay the edge of the side of the canvas to be bound on top of the tape, leaving half the width of the tape to turn over (Figure 1). Press the canvas firmly down onto the tape. Now turn the lower half of the tape up to cover the unbound side of the canvas. Make sure the masking tape sticks to the canvas by running the handle end of a pair of

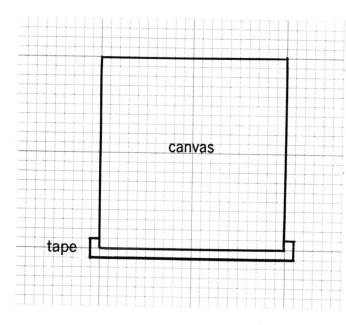

canvas

tape

Figure 1
Canvas edge on half width of
masking tape

dressmaking scissors back and forth across the tape on both sides of the canvas, applying heavy pressure. This process can be repeated if the tape should come loose while you are working on the canvas. Trim off any excess tape at the edges of the canvas, and bind all four sides in the same manner.

The tape will help prevent fraying along the edges of regular mono canvas. Although leno canvas does not fray, you will still want to bind the edges to prevent your clothes being snagged by the rough ends of cotton. The work itself can also be damaged if the rough edges of the canvas catch the wool as you roll up your work after sewing is finished for the day.

Yarn   The yarn used for all the projects in this book is three-ply Persian needlepoint and crewel wool. When working ten-mesh-to-one-inch canvas, the full three strands of the yarn are used. When using the finer eighteen-mesh-to-one-inch canvas, only two strands are used to cover the canvas properly and not distort the mesh during work. A standard rug wool is used for work on seven-mesh-to-one-inch mono canvas.

It is quite possible to substitute a standard four-ply wool knitting worsted, or any other four-ply yarn of the same weight and thickness, for the Persian wool when working on ten-mesh-to-one-inch canvas. Although not specifically designed for needlepoint, a good-quality knitting worsted covers the canvas well, giving a professional finish to work in straight stitches. Because knitting worsted is a lot less expensive than any needlepoint yarn, using it may well be a good setting-off point for the beginner. Those of you who have yarn left over from knitting or crochet projects may well be able to use up remnants when working designs from this book. For this reason I have given the approximate yardages to complete each design.

I have tried to be generous with the yarn allowances given for each project. It is very difficult indeed to gauge how much yarn the "average" person would use in working any given design. I myself tend to use a lot less yarn than most. The amount of yarn used depends on a multiplicity of factors: how long a thread you can happily work with, how much yarn you use up in starting and finishing off each length, how short a piece of yarn you are able to work with at the end of each thread, how tightly you pull your stitches, and so on.

My advice is that you purchase the yarn amounts given for each design and return any unused skeins to the shop when you have finished. Most needlework stores will take back unbroken skeins, provided they are of the same dye lot as current stock. The advantage of all the designs in this book is that they are very quick to make. You are therefore unlikely to have a piece of work hanging about the house for months on end in a semi-finished state.

If you do find, after working a design from this book, that the yarn amounts given are too generous for the way you work, this is likely to be true of all the other projects also, since the same standard has been applied throughout. You may well be able to cut down on the purchase of yarn for the next project you choose.

Persian needlepoint wool is available in many different yardages, such as 10- or 40-yard skeins, and a 4-ounce twisted hank. I have chosen to work with the smallest quantity, the 10-yard skein, in an attempt to cut down as much as possible on wastage. It is clear that if you need to use only a few sewing lengths from a new skein, you will be wasting far less cutting into a 10- than into a 40-yard skein. You will inevitably have some wastage, but considerably less. Some of the projects in the chapter on patchwork designs are ideal for using up scraps. You can utilize many more colors than those shown on the charts, making the charted squares the basis on which to create your own color combinations and patches.

Needles   You will need to use blunt-ended tapestry needles for this type of canvas work. Sharp needles should never be used, since they would pierce and split the yarn as you work one row on top of another. The size of needle will vary according to the canvas and yarn you are using. You must be able to thread the yarn through the eye of the needle without too much difficulty and be able to draw the threaded needle through the holes of the canvas without strain or distortion.

For ten-mesh-to-one-inch canvas with Persian needlepoint or knitted worsted wool, use a size 18 blunt-ended tapestry needle.

For eighteen-mesh-to-one-inch canvas with two strands only of Persian needlepoint wool, use a size 22 needle.

For seven-mesh-to-one-inch canvas and standard rug yarn, you will need a blunt-ended rug needle.

Miscellaneous   It is unlikely that you will ever need a frame for straight-stitch work. Unlike the diagonal needlepoint stitches, straight stitches do not distort the canvas. This is largely because the stitches are worked vertically, or occasionally horizontally, in the direction of the weave, and not at an angle to it. If you are used to working with a frame and want to continue doing so, there is no reason why you should not mount the canvas in the usual way and work accordingly. For those of you who, like me, prefer to carry your work around with you and do a few stitches whenever you have a spare moment, straight-stitch work will prove particularly pleasing. The canvas remains neat and clean during work if it is rolled up and placed, with the yarn, in a plastic bag while not in use. Do not be tempted to fold the canvas. This may well cause gaps to appear, particularly between vertical stitches, gaps that may be difficult to eradicate when pressing. Folding is also likely to cause distortions in the canvas, making those areas yet to be worked more difficult to cover when the time comes. This is especially true of the regular mono canvases.

You will find it useful to have a pair of sharp-pointed embroidery scissors to clip out any mistakes you may make, and to trim away the pieces of yarn that are left over at the ends of thread during work. If you are accustomed to using a thimble, then by all means continue to do so. However, it is not necessary to use one for this type of work, since the needles employed are rather large and blunt and unlikely to cause much damage to your fingers when being pushed or pulled through the canvas.

I find a 12-inch ruler, such as those children use at school, very useful for measuring yarn into equal and convenient sewing lengths. A piece of yarn wrapped once around the ruler, as shown in Figure 2, gives me a 24-inch length, which I find just right for sewing. In addition to this ruler you will also need a dressmaker's tape measure.

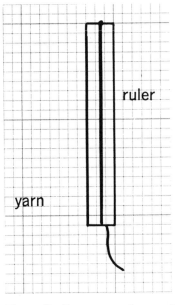

Figure 2 Yarn wrapped around a 12-inch ruler

Having assembled all the necessary tools for the job, you are now ready to embark on the sewing. Begin by cutting a length of yarn, using the wrap-around-the-ruler method shown in Figure 2. If you find that a 24-inch length is too long, and the yarn begins to fluff up or fray during work, try a shorter length. There is no "correct" length, just the most convenient length for you personally. However, I think it would be unwise to use lengths much greater than 24 inches, since the yarn is inevitably exposed to considerable wear and tear as it is pulled back and forth through the canvas. The longer the yarn, the more times

the stitches

the last section of it has been pulled back and forth. You would not want your project to look as if it had been exposed to years of wear before you have even finished it, which is what can easily happen with too long a piece of yarn.

On the other hand, if you cut the yarn too short, you will be forever starting and finishing off ends, a tiresome process that will also prove an extravagant waste of yarn. Try the 24-inch length and see how you manage with it. Minor adjustments of a few inches in either direction will then be possible later.

To begin work, thread the needle and bring it from the back to the front of the canvas in the correct starting mesh. Pull the yarn gently through the canvas until an end about 2 inches long remains at the back. The stitches will be worked from right to left across the canvas. Fold the end of yarn at the back of the canvas, from right to left across the back of the holes where the stitches will now be worked. Hold this end in place with the fingers of the hand not sewing and keep it slanting at a slight diagonal to the weave of the canvas, as shown in Figure 3. The first few stitches are worked over this end of yarn, so that it eventually disappears beneath the backs of the stitches you are going to make. The end of yarn is held at a slight slant upward from the bottom line of the stitches so that it does not interfere with the passage of the needle through the holes of the canvas.

When you reach the end of a piece of thread, take the yarn through to the back of the canvas in completing the last stitch. Weave in and out along the backs of the stitches already worked for a distance of about 2 inches (Photograph 2). Pull the yarn through and remove the needle. Trim off any excess yarn, taking care not to cut into the back of any of the stitches. As the canvas gradually becomes covered with stitches, you can start a piece of yarn by weaving it in and out along the backs of the stitches for about 2 inches, in the same way as for finishing.

Figure 3 End of yarn held at a diagonal

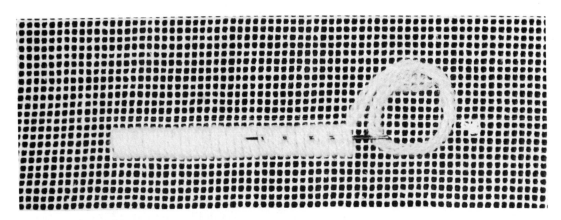

Photograph 2. Weaving in yarn at back of stitches

Upright Gobelin

This is the stitch that forms the basis of all projects in this book. Following the instructions given for starting and finishing lengths of yarn, work the stitch as follows:

STEP 1.   Bring the threaded needle through to the front of the work (Figure 4).

STEP 2.   Count up four holes, starting in the hole immediately above the place where the yarn comes through the canvas. Push the needle through to the back of the canvas by inserting it into the fourth hole counted (Figure 5). Pull the yarn gently through to the back of the canvas, taking care not to pull it too tight.

STEP 3.   Bring the needle up in the hole next to the bottom of the stitch you have just worked (Figure 6).

Repeat steps 2 and 3, working a row of stitches, side by side, in a straight line from right to left. It is not necessary to count the four holes for each stitch after the first, since you insert the needle into the hole next to the top of the stitch just worked. Figure 7 illustrates the order of the movements necessary to work several stitches side by side. Take care not to pull the yarn too tightly. The yarn should sit "comfortably" on the canvas,

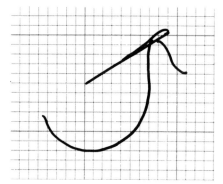

Figure 4 Threaded needle to front of work

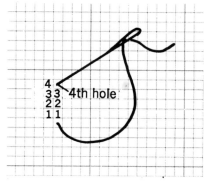

Figure 5 Needle into fourth hole

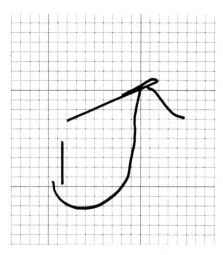

Figure 6 Needle into hole next to bottom hole of first stitch

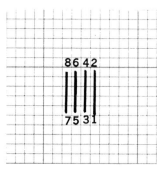

Figure 7 Moves for stitches side by side

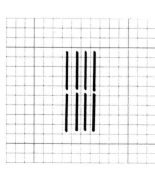

Figure 8 Row of stitches on top of another row

12

not pulling at the top and bottom of each stitch nor bagging out from the background of the canvas itself. You will get the feel of how tightly to draw the yarn after practicing the stitch a few times.

When you are ready to work a second row above the first, bring the needle up into the same hole as the top of the stitch in the row below, and repeat steps 2 and 3 as before (Figure 8).

The stitch just described is called upright Gobelin stitch worked over four holes or mesh of the canvas. Perhaps you have noticed that if you count the hole at which the stitch starts and finishes, you are actually working over five holes. Remember, though, that the top and bottom holes are shared by the lower and upper edges of the stitches on the rows above and below. Since you do count up four holes from the base of the stitch, it does, after all, seem logical to describe the stitch as being worked over four holes or mesh.

The stitches have been shown worked from right to left in the diagrams. There is no reason why you should not work from left to right if you find this direction more natural for you. If you do make this change, just be sure to start reading the charts, given with each project, in the same direction also. You will start working the chart, not as indicated by the arrow at the bottom right corner, but on the other side, at the bottom left corner.

It is possible to make upright Gobelin stitch shorter or longer by covering fewer or more mesh on the canvas. Figure 9 shows upright Gobelin stitch worked over two mesh of the canvas; Figure 10 shows it worked over six. Stitches longer than six mesh are generally unsatisfactory for work that is to be used as rugs, pillows, or indeed any item save those mounted on a board or poles for hanging. The large, unattached loops of yarn that result from making longer stitches are clearly impractical for use where people and things can become entangled in them.

When working upright Gobelin stitch over two holes of the canvas, a very rich texture is achieved, which is quite close in effect to that ordinarily created by diagonal-stitch needlepoint. One can obtain delicacy and detail without the attendant prob-

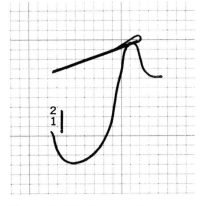

Figure 9 Working over two mesh

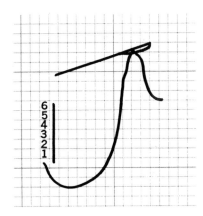

Figure 10 Working over six mesh

lem of distorting the canvas. Because it is worked over two mesh, it is still a lot quicker to complete than conventional needlepoint, and it certainly looks more like a woven fabric than upright Gobelin stitch over four mesh.

There is one problem that arises when working this finer stitch, but fortunately it is very simple to overcome. The yarn appears to twist considerably more when working over two holes than it does over four. If the yarn twists itself up too tightly, it will clearly become narrower and then will not be as effective in covering the background canvas. Gaps will begin to appear, not only between the rows of stitches, where a slight gap is inevitable, but also in a vertical direction, between the upright stitches themselves.

In order to prevent this happening, and to keep your yarn at its fullest and best covering width throughout, allow the yarn to hang free from the canvas and unwind itself after every few stitches, as shown in Figure 11. It is a good idea to repeat this

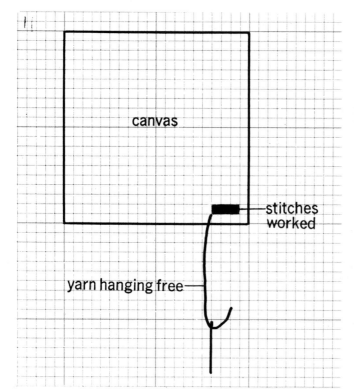

canvas

stitches worked

yarn hanging free

Figure 11
Yarn hanging free and unwinding

process as often as you may find necessary when working upright Gobelin stitch, even over four or six mesh if that seems appropriate.

With all upright stitches, coverage of the canvas is never as complete as it is with the diagonal stitches used for conventional needlepoint. One has to face this fact squarely from the start. A small space between the rows of stitches is unavoidable. Tiny flecks of canvas can be seen here and there even on the best-worked canvases. This factor is especially emphasized in fairly large areas worked in a dark color. However, much can be done to eliminate unsightly gaps by keeping the tension of your sewing just right, so that stitches lie flat and full on the canvas, covering as wide an area as possible. When stitches are pulled tightly, the yarn automatically thins out under the strain, and the result is a poorly covered canvas. Photograph 3 shows the correct and incorrect ways of working stitches and how these factors affect coverage.

**Photograph 3.
Correct and incorrect
coverage of canvas**

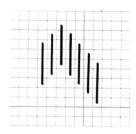

Figure 12 Slanting Gobelin over four mesh

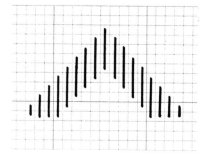

Figure 13 Graduated Gobelin

Figure 14 Bargello 4-2 step

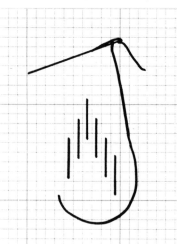

Unwinding the yarn during work, as described earlier, also helps tremendously in ensuring that the canvas is fully covered, and it may well make the difference between straggly, wispy stitches with ugly spaces between and the full-bodied stitches that make the finished piece such a pleasure to look at.

If you are not managing to cover the canvas well, check that you are not pulling the yarn too tightly and that it is not twisting up during work. If neither of these is the case, perhaps the yarn is too fine for the canvas, or the canvas too heavy for the yarn. Adjustments can be made by switching to a heavier yarn or finer canvas.

Graduated Gobelin Stitch

To make a slanting edge, begin each new stitch one mesh higher or lower than the one just worked (Figure 12).

To bring the stitches back into a straight line along the lower edge, they can be graduated, starting with a stitch worked over one mesh and increasing by one mesh each stitch until you are once again working over four mesh, as shown in Figure 13. Full-length slanting stitches can then be worked to create the desired pattern, returning to a straight edge by decreasing the length of stitches from four to one again (Figure 13).

Bargello Stitch

Bargello stitch is worked by beginning the next stitch either two mesh up or down from the original starting point of the previous stitch. Figure 14 shows Bargello stitch worked in a 4-2 step. Bargello stitch can also be worked in a 6-3 step when stitches of six-mesh length are being used.

Mistakes show up very quickly indeed in counted work and should be dealt with quickly and ruthlessly! Picking out stitches already worked proves unsatisfactory in canvas work, since the yarn thus retrieved will have passed through the canvas three times in all, instead of the usual once. For this reason it is best to clip out mistakes, using a pair of sharp-pointed embroidery scissors. Cut the stitches at the halfway point on the front of the work, so that you can see just how many have to come out. Take care not to cut into the canvas as you do this. Gently lift the stitches out along the back of the work, using your tapestry needle to help you. Clear away all ends of yarn and start with a fresh thread.

If you should be unfortunate enough to clip the canvas by mistake, take a thread from the side of the canvas and weave it across the tear for a few mesh on either side. You will be able to work over the cut in the usual manner and clip away any excess thread at the same time.

Once you have mastered these simple stitches, you will be ready for the next stage, which is reading the charts.

following the charts

Following a chart is not at all difficult, once you understand a few simple rules. If you have a problem "seeing" a chart clearly, then there are some helpful suggestions I should like to make right at the start. The charts in this book are all presented on graph paper, and because of the limitations of space, they appear in a considerably scaled-down version of the piece of needlework they are supposed to represent. The charts can very easily, and inexpensively, be blown up to a much larger size.

All you need to do this is a cheap arithmetic notebook, printed in squares. This type of children's arithmetic book is available in almost any five-and-dime store. Having selected the design you want to make, you can copy the chart, square by square, onto the larger squared arithmetic paper. You could use the color symbols that I have given on the chart. Again, these symbols appear as a matter of necessity rather than choice. To reproduce every chart in color would make the book impossibly expensive. However, you can produce your own colored charts simply by using crayons, magic markers, or colored pencils, or any combination of the three. After all, this chart is for your own personal use and does not have to look like a work of art, or even be particularly neat, as long as you are able to follow it.

When you have chosen the yarn colors you are going to use for your design, try to match your markers to these colors. Then fill in the pattern in color, square by square. You now have an enlarged chart with the correct colors of your own choice to follow as you sew. The very act of making one of these copy charts for yourself should take away most of the mystery, and all of the fear, which for some reason persists when it comes to charted and counted work. What you have drawn is a larger, colored representation of the chart as it appears on the page in the book. One of the large squares on your arithmetic paper equals one of the smaller squares on the graph. If you have chosen to use color, then one of your colored squares represents one of the squares on the graph marked by a symbol such as a dot, circle, or cross. The next step is to "translate" your chart into needlepoint stitches. This is just as easy as the first step. For those of you who have no fear of charts, are able to follow symbols easily, and find the charts in the book sufficiently large for your eyes, this preliminary step will not, of course, be necessary. You can proceed directly to the charts provided.

Many of the charts given in the project section have their starting point indicated by an arrow in the lower right corner. These charts are worked row by row upward from the bottom line. Your starting point on the canvas, which corresponds to the arrow on the chart, should be measured 2 inches up from the bottom and in from the right edge of the canvas.

With every graph in the book there is a key to what each square represents in terms of stitches on the canvas. Let us take an example: "One square on chart = 4 stitches and 4 holes on the canvas." If you are following a chart like this, it means that for each square that you see on the chart you must make a block of four stitches worked over four mesh of the canvas. This block of stitches is illustrated in Figure 15. The square on the chart is now being represented by a "square" or "block" of four stitches on the canvas. Each square on the chart is "translated" into stitches on the canvas in this manner.

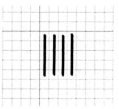

Figure 15
Block of four stitches

If you feel that you are likely to become confused as to how many squares on the chart you have actually worked as blocks of stitches on the canvas, there is a simple remedy. Make a copy chart for your own use, as described earlier in this chapter. With a heavy black marker, cross off each square on your chart as you put it down on the canvas. Not only will this help you to follow the chart accurately, but it will also ensure that you obtain the correct number of stitches to be worked when there are large areas of the canvas to be sewn in the same color.

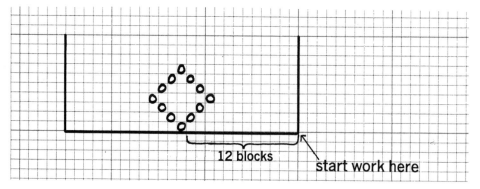

Figure 16 Sample chart

Take, for example, the imaginary chart shown in Figure 16. On the bottom row of the chart, where work is to begin, you have twelve squares in the background color before you reach the contrasting shade. Each square represents four stitches, so we know that there are forty-eight stitches (twelve squares multiplied by four stitches) to be worked before we reach the one square (four stitches) in the contrasting color. It is a tiresome nuisance to keep counting stitches, yet, in order to achieve accurate results with counted work, it is often necessary to do so. Fortunately, there are a few tricks by which you can minimize the amount of counting you do. If you are going to cross off each square of four stitches on your chart as you work them, you will not have to keep counting the stitches or squares as you go along. When the last square is crossed off in the background shade, you are ready to change color. You should count the stitches once at this point, just to double-check that you have indeed worked the correct number, forty-eight.

For those of you who do not wish to make use of subsidiary charts and who are quite prepared to do some counting in the course of working these designs, there is a useful method of cutting down counting time that you may like to use. If you are working on ten-mesh-to-one-inch canvas and following the imaginary chart shown in Figure 16, you can easily calculate how long, in terms of inches, forty-eight stitches will be. Dividing forty-eight (the number of stitches) by ten (the number of mesh to an inch), we can calculate that the first side of the bottom

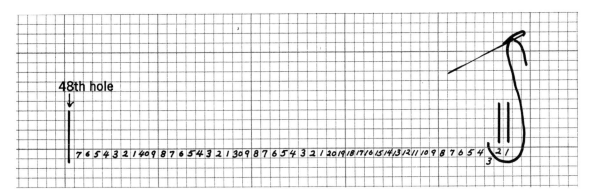

Figure 17 Vertical mark for stitch count

row, worked in the background color, is just two holes short of 5 inches. You can quickly measure the stitches when you think you are nearing the 5-inch mark. When you are just under 5 inches, count the stitches only once to check that you have the correct number. Measuring the stitches in this way avoids the necessity of counting each stitch as it is worked, something that may be highly impractical when interruptions are likely!

Yet a third shortcut to counting stitches exists. Work a couple of stitches in the background color. Using your needle to count each hole, work your way along the row until forty-eight mesh have been counted. Remember to include in your count the first few stitches you have already worked. When the needle is resting in the forty-eighth mesh, mark this with a permanent marker in a vertical direction as shown in Figure 17. Now continue working stitches along the row in the usual manner until you reach the marked stitch. As you cover this mark, you will be working the last stitch in that color.

If you intend to use this method of counting, I urge you always to use permanent markers when drawing any lines on the canvas, no matter how small and insignificant they may appear to be. Color from water-based markers may run into the yarn to spoil your work during steaming and blocking. I also advise against the use of pencils, since particles of graphite cling to the canvas, are transferred to the yarn during work, and can make light colors look dirty, a most undesirable side effect!

I have deliberately chosen an "awkward" design for my

21

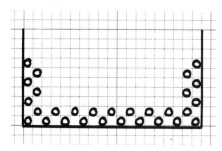

Figure 18
Simple border pattern in alternating blocks

sample chart, to illustrate the worst counting problems that may arise. In most cases, designs have a border pattern with alternating blocks of two or more colors, where very little counting is necessary. Figure 18 shows just such a border pattern. Starting work in the usual manner, at a point 2 inches up from the lower and in from the side edge of the canvas, sew the first block of four stitches represented by the circle on the chart. The next block of stitches is worked in the background shade. It would be very tiresome, and extremely wasteful in terms of yarn, to finish off colors after every four stitches. To avoid this, count along four mesh from the last stitch worked, and bring the needle up into the fifth hole, as shown in Figure 19. You have left a space for the block in the background color to be filled in later.

Continue along the row, leaving spaces where indicated on the chart, until all the blocks marked on the chart by a circle have been worked on the canvas. Return to the first space, and fill that in with the background color. Fill in all the spaces in this manner. When working the second row of the border pattern, you simply work the blocks marked by a circle above each block in the background color, and vice versa. No counting at all is necessary. If Figure 18 were a completed design, you would simply continue working up the chart, row by row, until the pattern is complete.

It is quite permissible to "jump" across four stitches or mesh in the manner just described. However, if the border were like that shown in Figure 20, with two squares in the background

Figure 19   Skipping a four-stitch block

5th hole

4 3 2 1

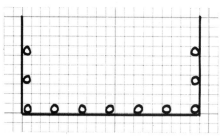

Figure 20
Blocks of one and two in a border pattern

color between each contrasting square, it would be advisable to work the wider blocks first. When filling in the spaces left for the contrasting color, do not jump across the eight stitches worked in the background shade. It is not necessary to finish off the contrasting color and begin again for each separate block. Instead, the yarn can be woven in and out across the back of the eight stitches to be jumped, as if you were going to finish off the end of yarn (see Photograph 2, page 11). Instead of cutting the yarn, bring the needle through to the front of the work, in the correct hole for filling in the next space in the contrasting color.

Weaving the yarn across the backs of other stitches in this way avoids the necessity of constantly starting and finishing yarn, wherever distance separates two blocks worked in the same color. Cutting and finishing the yarn too frequently could easily cause a bulkiness in the finished canvas and could even result in visible lumps in what should be a smoothly woven appearance.

Although most canvas work will be mounted or backed in some way, it is never wise to jump across more than a few stitches without weaving in the yarn. Unattached loops of yarn may well be covered in the finishing process, but the main argument against the practice of taking long jumps across the back of the work is that it is difficult to control the tension of the yarn across a wide stretch. You may pull too tightly, in which case you will almost certainly make the yarn tighter than the canvas it is supposed to rest upon. This results in a visibly wrinkled canvas, or one that simply refuses to come into shape at the final pressing. On the other hand, if you leave the loops of yarn too loose across the back, the stitches worked before and after the jump was taken tend to work themselves loose as you work, or as the finished item is put to use. This gives rise to an uneven tension in the stitches and does not enhance the appearance of the finished piece.

Some of the charts in this book begin in the center square instead of at the lower right corner. This is always the case where the lower portion of the design is filled in with several rows of stitches in the same color. Counting stitches across the entire width of the canvas would be tedious and quite unnecessary where starting at the center would simplify the sewing. Find the center square on the chart by tracing down the center line indicated at the top and across the center line indicated at the side. The square in which these two lines meet is the center of the design. If you are making your own enlarged chart, as described earlier in this chapter, start copying the design from the center square instead of from the edge as you did before. Outline this center square in a contrasting color so that it will be clearly visible when you have completed your copy chart.

In order to start work on the design, it is also necessary to find the center of the canvas. To do this, fold the canvas in half lengthwise and mark the fold, across the center, with a permanent ink marker, drawing a line about 4 inches long in the middle of the canvas. Now fold the canvas in half again, this time along the width, and mark as before. The mesh in which the two lines cross is the center hole of the canvas (Figure 21).

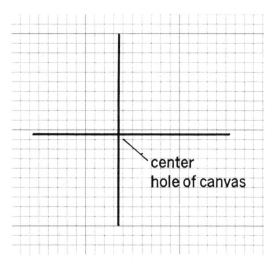
center
hole of canvas

Figure 21   Marking the center of
the canvas

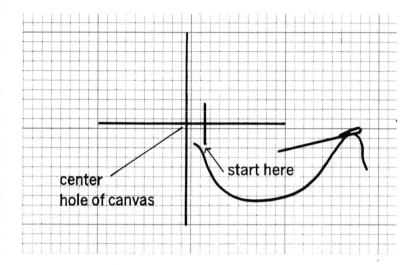

center
hole of canvas

start here

Figure 22
Working the center block

To work the center square of the chart in the center of the canvas, start the first block of stitches two holes to the right of and two holes below the center mesh, as shown in Figure 22. Follow the charted design across the row, from right to left, until the left edge is reached. Figure 23 shows a completed design with the first line "extracted," showing how the first row is worked from the center square to the left side of the pattern. Complete the rest of the first row by working the stitches from left to right, from the center square, until you reach the right edge of the design.

If you find that working from left to right is awkward and slows down your sewing too much, simply turn the canvas around and begin working the design from right to left again. With symmetrical designs this may be done without turning the chart, since both sides of the design are the same. It is unlikely that you will be starting an asymmetrical design in the center, but should this ever be the case, make sure that you turn the chart as you turn the canvas. It would be a good idea to mark the chart "top" and "bottom" before you start work. It is easy enough to see which way a chart should be when working from a

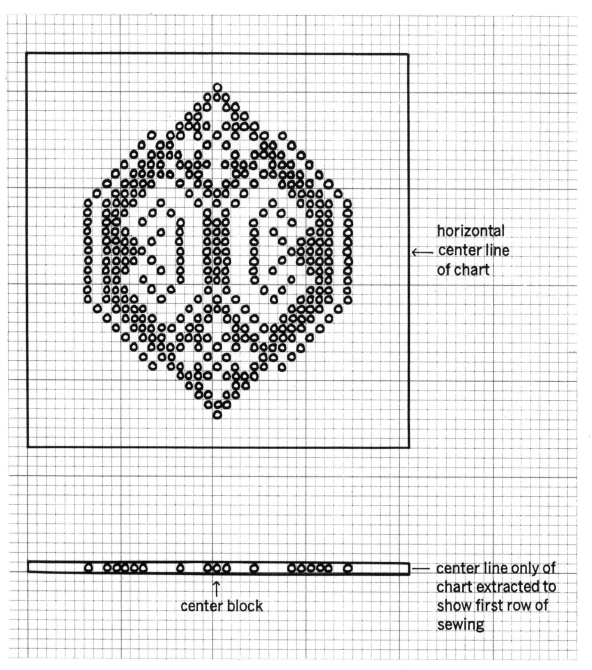

horizontal
← center line
of chart

center line only of
chart extracted to
show first row of
sewing

↑
center block

Figure 23 Design plus center line extracted

book, but it is important to mark the top and bottom if you are working from your own drawings. The canvas should be marked in the same way, with a permanent ink marker, before you begin sewing. By using this simple method, you will always know which part of the chart you should be following, however many times you turn the canvas around for the convenience of working the stitches in the direction you find most natural.

Now that the center horizontal line of stitches is complete, you can continue working the design in rows across, just as you would for a design that you start in the right-hand corner. Work all the rows above the center line, following the chart. Then complete the canvas by working all the rows below the center line. Even designs started in the center of the canvas are easy to work once the center square has been found and the center block of stitches established on the canvas. However, since there are a few more steps involved before work can begin, I have not recommended any of these designs for the absolute beginner.

Thus far we have chosen our examples from designs in which the stitches are worked over four mesh of the canvas. If the key at the top of the chart says, "One square on chart = 2 stitches and 2 holes on the canvas," then the building blocks of stitches are two stitches, side by side, worked over two mesh of the canvas, as shown in Figure 24.

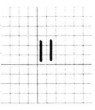

Figure 24
Block of two stitches

If the key at the top of the chart says, "One square on chart = 6 stitches and 6 holes on the canvas," then the block is six stitches side by side, each stitch worked over six mesh of the canvas, as shown in Figure 25.

This discussion brings me to an important point I should like to make about the projects in this book. For the beginner, I suggest choosing from those designs designated as suitable in the project section, making them up into straightforward items such as those outlined in Chapter 3. However, for those of you with more experience, and an adventurous spirit, I suggest using these designs, particularly the squares, as building blocks from which to create your own individual projects. To help you

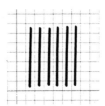

Figure 25
Block of six stitches

use the charts in as many ways as possible, I include in this chapter some useful information on how to enlarge or reduce designs and transform the simple squares into rugs, wall hangings, floor cushions, and so on.

Any design in the book that is worked over four mesh can be halved in size by treating each square as if it represented two stitches and two holes on the canvas instead of four. If the finished size of the canvas is given as 16 x 16 inches when it is worked over four mesh, it would measure 8 x 8 inches when worked over two. The same design can be increased in size by working over six mesh instead of four. This would make the finished canvas half as big again as the original piece, 24 x 24 inches in this example. Proportionate adjustments should also be made in the amounts of yarn required for the project. Altering the length of the stitches used and changing the "value" of the squares on the charts make it easy and fun to change any design to suit your own requirements.

Alterations can also be made by changing the yarn and canvas used. Any of the designs worked with Persian needlepoint wool on ten-mesh-to-one-inch canvas can be enlarged by changing to a standard rug yarn and seven-mesh-to-one-inch canvas, while keeping the length of the stitches the same as those indicated on the chart. A square that measured 14 x 14 inches when worked in the original materials would measure approximately 20 x 20 inches on rug canvas. A 16-inch square would measure approximately 23 x 23 inches when altered in the same way. When working a 20-inch square on rug canvas, you need approximately 220 yards of yarn to cover the canvas, and about 300 yards for a 24-inch square. This method of enlarging a design is ideal when the change to rug yarn is compatible with the use of the finished item. Any rug that has to withstand wear and tear on the floor would be more sensibly worked in a substantial rug yarn.

Some rugs fulfill a decorative rather than a utilitarian function. For such rugs as these, and for wall hangings, Persian wool and finer canvas can be used. Try using the many squares provided to make interesting patterns of your own creation. You can make very attractive rugs or wall hangings by working different patterned squares of the same size and sewing them together afterward. Figure 26 shows how two such 14-inch squares can be joined together to make a larger panel. The dimensions of the rug or wall hanging would be approximately 28 x 42 inches.

By using these squares as flexible building blocks for creating larger projects, you can determine the final dimensions by arranging the squares according to your requirements. It is best to plot out the final assembly of pieces on graph paper before you begin sewing. This ensures that the patterns you have selected to mix and match do indeed blend together to create the effect you have in mind.

It is possible to work the rug or hanging all in one piece, treating your chart of the assembled squares as one continuous fabric. If you decide to do this, start work in the lower right corner, just as you would normally do for working a single square. The great advantage of working the squares as if they were tiles, and joining them together afterward, is that they are individually much more portable than a larger expanse of canvas. You also have the added bonus of being able to work rugs and wall hangings in sizes larger than the standard widths of canvas available at your needlework store.

By working in squares you can build up a rug, section by section, without ever feeling that you have embarked on an enormous and daunting undertaking. From personal experience I have found that several small squares, making up the ground area of a large rug, are finished much more quickly than the same area of canvas worked in one continuous strip. Apart from the psychological advantage of having smaller pieces, each of which when completed spurs you on to finish the larger project, there are distinct practical gains from working in smaller sections. Squares are more portable and therefore more work gets done during odd free moments. A large roll of canvas can be extremely cumbersome to work with. As you fill in more and more of the design, the weight of the yarn becomes an additional factor in making the work heavy and difficult to manage. However, it remains a matter of individual choice which method of working appeals to you most.

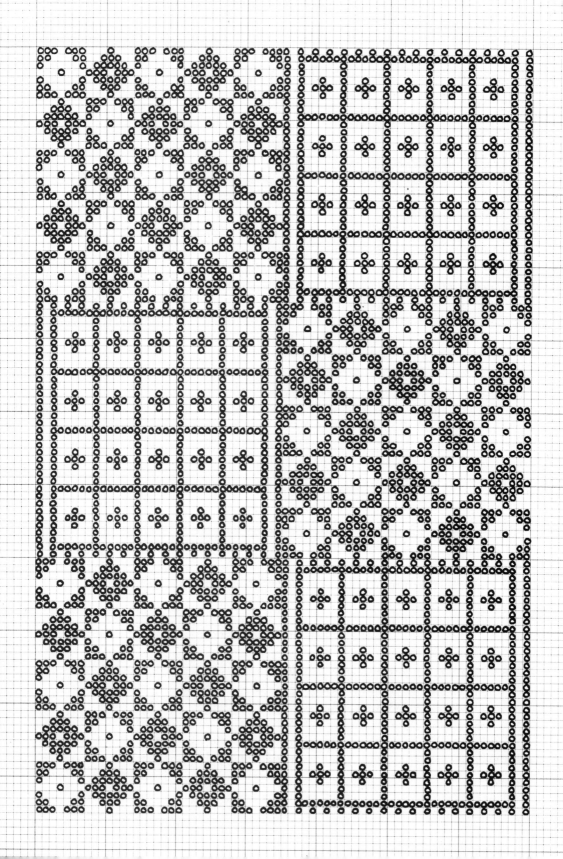

Let me suggest a few other ways in which you might care to make use of the squares in the project section. When you have a design that looks different when turned on its side, try alternating the pattern, as shown in Figure 27. You could also use a plain square to break up squares of pattern, as indicated in Figure 28. When it comes to choosing colors for a project, bear in mind that some interesting contrasting effects can be achieved by reversing the background and main colors on a chart where only two colors are used. Figure 29 shows how colors make the changes in a rug or wall hanging, where the same pattern square is used throughout.

I hope you will experience creative enjoyment when using the squares in this book in your own individual way. Remember that it is always best to map out your completed design on graph paper before you start sewing. Decide if you are going to make the project in one strip or in separate squares, and calculate the yarn and canvas you will require. For working a plain square, add up the yarn amounts given for the colors in a patterned square of the same size. Deduct one 10-yard skein from the total. If you are repeating the same square several times in a rug and using the same colors each time, you will require less yarn than if you were to make the squares in different colors on each occasion. After working one square, you will have yarn left over with which to begin the next. The best plan may be to ask your needlework store if they will put aside the total amount of yarn in the colors you need. After working the first square, you will be able to see how much residue there is in each color and reduce your yarn order accordingly. You will then be able to return unwanted skeins while the same dye lot is still in stock at the store.

You can also make use of the squares in the project section to create matching pillows to complement your rugs and wall hangings. Should you want to make a floor cushion in rug-weight canvas and yarn, using one of the charts given for finer materials, please refer to the size conversions given earlier in this chapter. If you choose a 14-inch square worked on ten-mesh-to-one-inch canvas, for example, this would create a 20-inch

Figure 26   Two-patterned rug or wall hanging

31

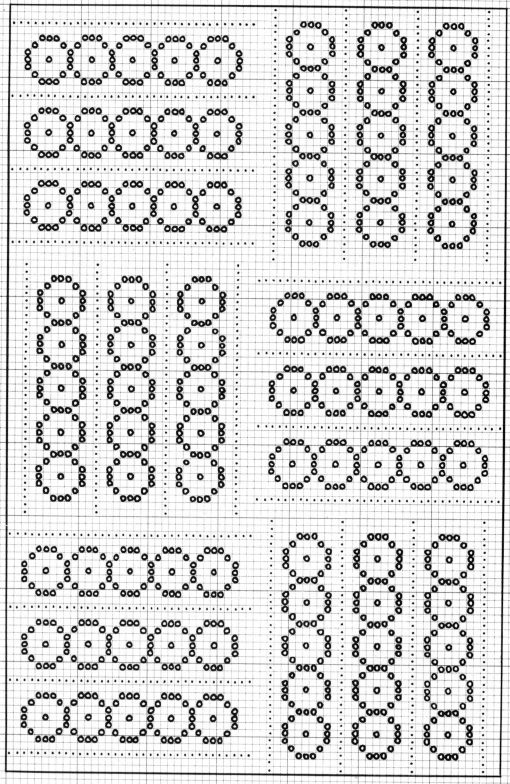

Figure 27　Pattern turned on its side

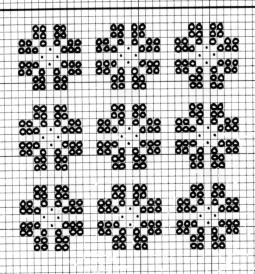

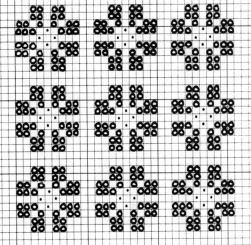

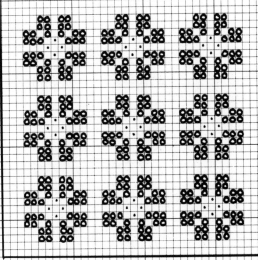

Figure 28 Plain and patterned squares

33

square on rug canvas. Suppose that you want the finished dimensions of the floor cushion to be 24 x 24 inches; how can you achieve this? The answer is simple. A border pattern can be added to the basic chart to bring the finished canvas up to the required size.

Bearing in mind that one square on the chart equals four stitches on the canvas, and that seven mesh on the canvas is equal to 1 inch, you will need to add three additional squares at each side of the chart to add the additional 2 inches to each side of the design. Two inches on the canvas equal precisely fourteen holes. Three squares on the chart equal twelve stitches. By adding three additional squares to the basic chart you achieve a finished size of just under 24 x 24 inches. If you add another square to each side, you obtain a finished measurement of just over 24 x 24 inches. Figure 30 shows how you can add two such borders to a simple design to increase the size. It is important to remember when adding borders to a basic square that whatever you do to one side of a pattern, you must also do to the others. This keeps the design at the center of the finished piece. Follow this simple rule, unless you are deliberately striving for an asymmetrical effect. Figure 31 shows how not to apply additional squares to a design, creating a lopsided look that does nothing to enhance this particular pattern.

Borders, such as those just described, are easy to apply to any design, provided that the addition is thoroughly worked out on graph paper before work is begun. If you want to use wider border panels at any time, you may wish to create your own patterns on a graph, or make use of some of the cushion strip designs illustrated in the project section. Once again, any alterations should be properly explored on paper before sewing.

Having mastered the amazingly simple art of charting designs on graph paper before setting to work, an almost limitless collection of designs becomes available for you to transfer to canvas. You can make copies of your favorite geometric designs, or even map out a section from a patterned rug or carpet in your home that you would like to use as the basis for a complementary wall hanging or pillow. Working over two mesh of the

Figure 29   Squares with colors reversed

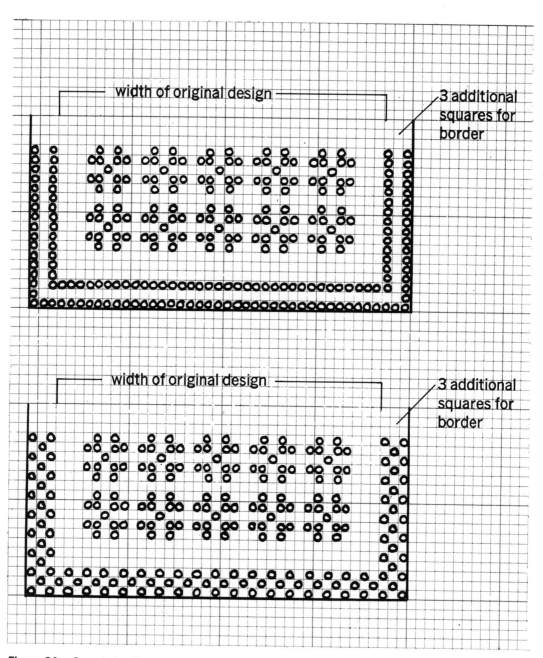

Figure 30 Sample borders

36

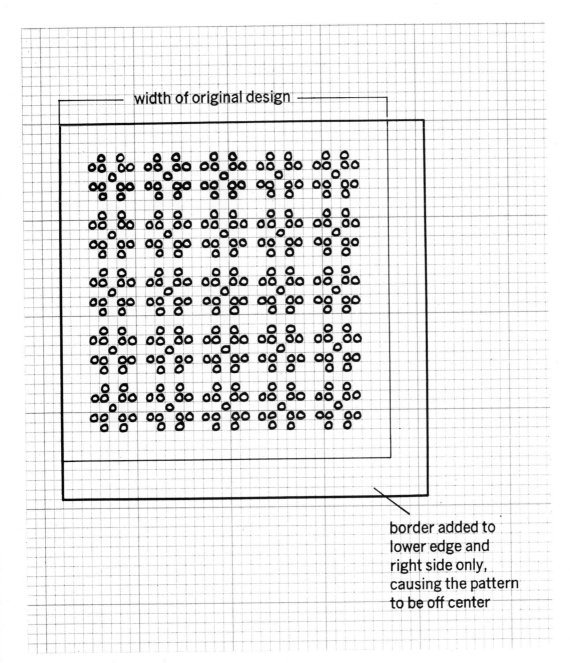

width of original design

border added to
lower edge and
right side only,
causing the pattern
to be off center

Figure 31 Lopsided addition of squares

canvas in upright Gobelin stitch can create effects almost as subtle and detailed as diagonal-stitch needlepoint. The great advantage of working in upright stitches is that you can carry your work around with you, without risking a terrible distortion of the canvas that would require hours of patient blocking and steaming to put right. Nor do you have to be a good artist to work out your own creative ideas on canvas. Mapping out a design on a graph is so much easier than drawing freehand on a blank sheet of paper. Once the design is down on the graph, it is so simple to interpret it on the canvas.

Yarn amounts for your own projects can easily be calculated. Cut a yard length of the yarn you will be using. Cut the 36-inch lengths into two 18-inch pieces. On the canvas you intend to use for the project, working in the stitch length you have selected, make a row of stitches, using up both lengths of yarn. Start and finish each thread in the usual manner. Count the number of stitches you have worked. Let us say, for the sake of example, that it is forty. If you are going to work in blocks of four stitches over four holes of the canvas, a yard of yarn will cover ten squares on the chart (forty divided by four). If you are using blocks of two stitches and two holes, a yard covers twenty squares (forty divided by two). If you want to use blocks of six stitches and six holes, a yard covers six blocks plus four stitches. Whenever you have a number of stitches left over when making these calculations, always correct *down* to the nearest full block of stitches covered. By observing this practice, and by working with a shorter length of yarn than usual, you should ensure that you have enough yarn to finish the project. It is always better to err on the generous side with your amounts, since dye lots can vary.

Now that you know how many squares on the chart a yard of yarn will cover, count how many blocks in each color you will have to work for your chosen design. An easy way to do this is to enter the total figure for separate colors on each line of the graph, as shown in Figure 32. Totals for the numbers of squares worked in the color represented by a circle appear on the right

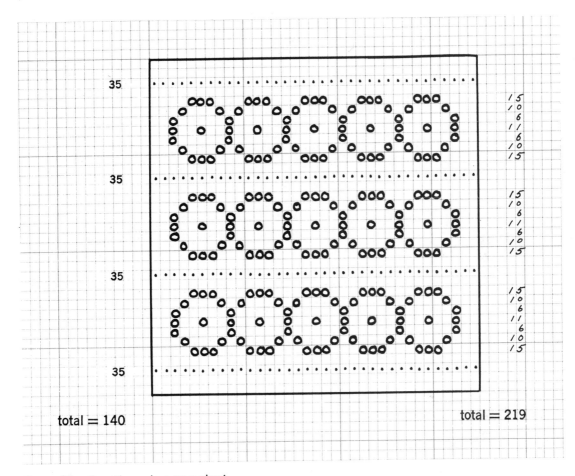

Figure 32 Counting colors on a chart

side for each row in which that color occurs. Figures for the second color, represented by a dot, appear on the left. Add up the columns of figures on each side. Divide these numbers by the number of blocks covered by 1 yard of yarn. You have now calculated how many yards of yarn you will require in each of the two contrasting shades. Always correct *up* to the next yard if there are any blocks left over after division. This allows a little extra yarn again.

To find out how many yards are needed in the background color on our sample chart, we must first calculate the total number of squares in the design. The chart is 35 squares wide and the same number of squares deep. By multiplying 35 by 35 we reach the total number of squares, which is 1,225 in this example. From this figure deduct the totals of the squares to be worked in different colors, 140 and 219 in this case. We are left with a total of 866 squares in the background shade. Divide this figure by the number of squares covered by 1 yard of yarn, and correct up to the nearest yard as before.

This method of calculation can be applied to any charted design. It takes a little time, but will save you money in the long run by helping you to avoid purchasing excessive quantities of yarn when branching out into your own creative projects.

the finishing touches

It is well worth taking a little extra time and trouble to make your finished work look neat and professional. In this chapter you will find general instructions for ways to enhance any piece of needlepoint worked in upright stitches, plus details of how to make your finished canvases into a number of attractive and useful items.

general hints

When worked in straight stitches, the canvas is not subject to the same kind of distortion one would find after making a needlepoint project in one of the diagonal stitches. Nevertheless, the finished work may well look crumpled and a little less than straight-edged. This can be the case no matter how carefully you have rolled up the canvas after each session of working on it. However, there is no need to spend time and energy with elaborate blocking techniques. You can "ease" your canvas back into shape with the help of a steam iron, or a regular iron with an old, but clean, piece of sheeting dampened in water. Be sure to remove any masking tape and to clip away ends of yarn before you begin work. You want to handle the canvas as little as possible once it is in shape.

If you are using a steam iron, place the finished canvas face down on an ironing table and spray jets of steam over the work until it is thoroughly dampened. *Never put the iron directly on the canvas.* While the piece is still warm, smooth out the surface and pull any uneven edges gently back into shape with your hands. When all the sides seem to be straightened out, turn the canvas over so that the right side of the work is now facing you, and apply some more steam. Give a final smoothing and shaping while the canvas is still damp and warm.

The yarn will retain moisture after the steaming. To dry the work, carefully lift it onto a clean, flat surface to air. Moisture may well collect under the canvas, so it is best to place it on a water-resistant surface of some kind, such as a plastic-coated table. When the top of the canvas appears dry to the touch, turn it over to air the other side. Wipe away any beads of moisture that may have collected underneath. *Never hang a canvas on a line to dry.* By doing so you will undo all the good work of shaping and smoothing under the steam.

Those of you who do not possess a steam iron need not despair. The process can be accomplished just as easily with an ordinary iron. You will need a square of clean, old sheeting material, several inches larger all around than the canvas itself. Soak the cloth in cold water and wring out as much water as possible by hand. Place the canvas face down on your ironing table. If possible, give extra padding to your ironing surface by placing some towels under a top cover of old sheeting. This helps to reduce the pressure on the stitches and to prevent the canvas acquiring a "flattened" look.

Lay the dampened cloth over the canvas. Select a high heat for the iron, either the "cotton" or "linen" setting. Pass the iron back and forth across the canvas with light pressure. Steam will begin to rise from the cloth and to penetrate the canvas below. When you have ironed over the entire surface, peel back the dampened cloth and gently smooth and pull the canvas into shape with your hands, while it is still warm and damp. You can repeat this process as many times as appear to be necessary. Keep the canvas with the right side facing down. Since pressure must be applied to the canvas when using this method, it is advisable to restrict this to the back of the work. Do not be tempted to use pounding strokes when "ironing" the canvas. The idea is to create a penetrating steam by means of a damp cloth. Moisten the cloth again when it appears to be drying out, and under no circumstances apply a hot iron directly to the canvas.

Either of these methods can be satisfactorily used when the canvas has been made into a finished item. It will probably be necessary to steam only the seams, and not the entire canvas again.

Trim the canvas to within ½ inch of the embroidery stitches all around. Cut a piece of backing fabric exactly the same size as the canvas (including its ½-inch margin of unworked canvas). Place the canvas and backing with right sides together, and machine stitch as shown in Figure 33, leaving a gap at the bottom edge. When machine stitching, keep the canvas side of the work facing up and sew into the hole where the last embroidery stitch was worked. This ensures that no ugly border of canvas will show around the edge of the pillow. Following the

making a pillow

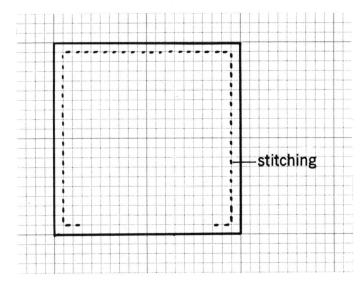

stitching

Figure 33
Stitching a pillow

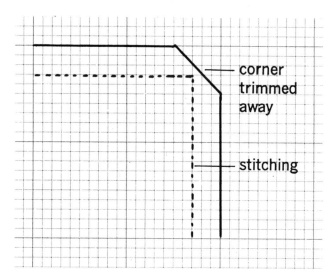

corner
trimmed
away

stitching

Figure 34
Trimmed corner of canvas
and fabric

line of the canvas also helps to keep the machine stitching absolutely straight. Trim away the excess canvas and fabric across the corners, to avoid bulkiness (Figure 34).

Now turn the pillow right side out through the space at the bottom. With the blunt end of a pencil, knitting needle, or crochet hook, ease the corners into shape. Do not use sharp instruments, such as a pair of scissors, for this purpose. You could very easily damage the canvas, or cause the canvas to work free from the backing where the joining is at its weakest. Gently steam all the seams.

Insert a cushion pad through the space left at the bottom of the pillow cover. Turn under the unworked margin of the canvas and the ½-inch seam allowance of the backing fabric. Pin these edges together. With a blending thread, close the gap by over-sewing the edge of the canvas to the edge of the backing fabric.

Decorative touches such as tassels and piping should be applied to the canvas before joining it to the backing fabric. If you are not familiar with the techniques of making covered pipe cord in the same fabric as the backing, I suggest that you pur-

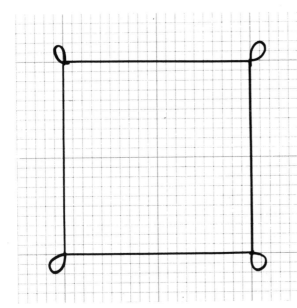

Figure 35
Looped corner trim

chase some ready-made decorative piping, which can be sewn onto the pillow by hand after it is completed. You can easily calculate the length you require by measuring around the entire perimeter of the pillow. If you would like to add a decorative loop of piping at each corner, as shown in Figure 35, then add about 3 inches extra for each loop.

mounting a picture

You can, of course, have your finished tapestries mounted and framed professionally. If, like me, you have a large number of pieces you wish to display, the thought of the expense involved in mounting and framing can be very discouraging indeed. For this reason I have found a simple way of mounting canvas on a board, which is inexpensive and easy to do.

you will need

▶ A piece of wood or hardboard not more than ¼ inch thick, cut to size to measure ¼ inch less in width and length than the embroidered area of the canvas

▶ An upholsterer's staple gun

This is a fairly expensive piece of equipment if you are going to use it for mounting only one canvas. However, as soon as you start using it on a few more projects, it will quickly pay for itself in money saved on professional mounting and framing. It is a handy tool to have around the house for other jobs as well, so it can be considered a worthwhile investment.

▶ A piece of string or cord to be attached to the back of the picture

Since this cord will be out of sight, it does not have to be anything fancy, as long as it is strong. The length should be about the width of the finished area of the canvas. You will also probably need the help of another person to help you hold the canvas in position as you staple.

METHOD

1. Double over each end of the string or cord for about 1 inch. Apply it to the back of the board, as shown in Figure 36, and staple it in place.

2. Having smoothed and shaped the canvas as described at the beginning of this chapter, trim the canvas borders to within 1 inch of the embroidery and place the piece, face down, on a work table. If you do not want staple marks to scar the surface of the table, make sure that you cover it with an old blanket or a couple of old, thick towels.

3. Place the board on top of the canvas so that there is an equal border of canvas on all sides (Figure 37).

4. Fold over the top edge of the canvas and staple it in the center and at a 2-inch distance on each side (Figure 38).

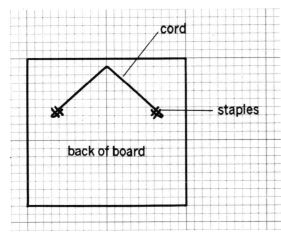

Figure 36
Applying cord to back of a picture

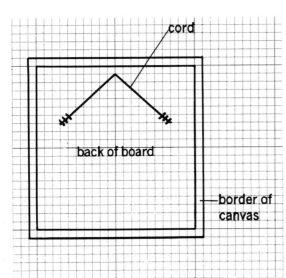

Figure 37
Board positioned on top of canvas

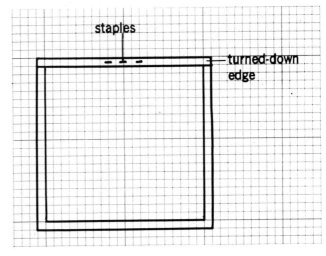

Figure 38
Starting the stapling

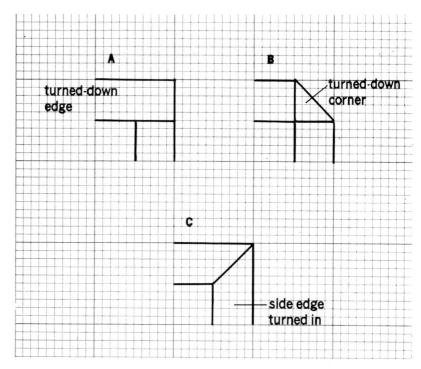

Figure 39
Mitering
a corner

turned-down edge

A

turned-down corner

B

C

side edge turned in

5. Do the same to the opposite, bottom edge, making sure that the canvas is pulled taut across the back of the board.

6. Fix the remaining side edges in the same manner, making certain that the canvas is quite smooth and taut.

7. Miter each of the four corners, as shown in Figure 39, and staple them in position.

8. Add more staples along all sides as necessary to secure a smooth finish.

The picture is now ready to be hung. You can crochet a trim in a matching color to put around the edge of the canvas, rather like a frame. This would add a neat finishing touch but is by no means necessary.

This technique is used in so many of the finished items that appear in the book that it will save time to describe it here in full and once only. Refer back to these instructions whenever this method is used for a specific project.

turning and finishing the edges of a canvas

METHOD

1. Having smoothed and straightened the canvas as described earlier in this chapter, place the work face down on a flat surface.
2. Trim the canvas to a width of 1 inch of unworked margin on all sides (Figure 40).
3. Fold down the top 1-inch border of canvas along the line created by the last row of the sewing, bringing the margin of unworked canvas to the back of the piece (Figure 41). Pin in place, but leave the side margin unpinned.

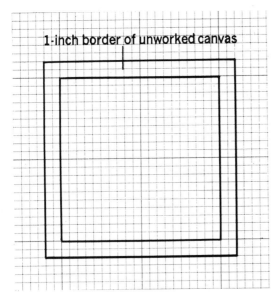

Figure 40   Canvas with unworked border

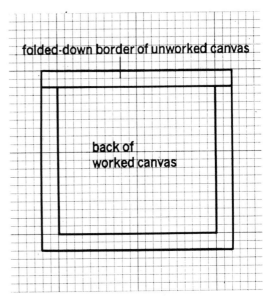

Figure 41   Turning in the edges

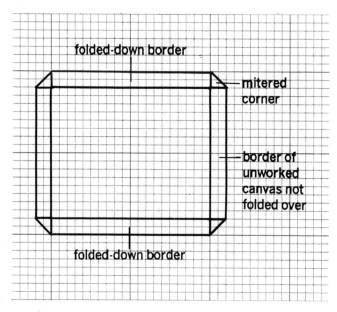

Figure 42 Mitering the corners

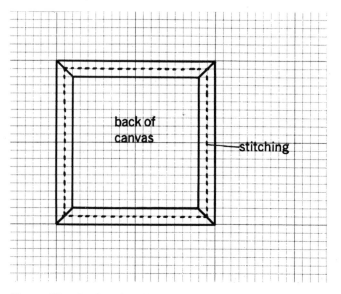

Figure 43 Sewing the edges in place

4. Fold and pin the opposite side, the lower edge in this case, in the same manner.
5. Miter the corners, as shown in Figure 42.
6. Fold in the side edges and pin in place.
7. Using a sharp-pointed needle and white cotton, tack around the edges, about ¼ inch up from the lower edge of the turned canvas. Sew with long running stitches, removing pins as you go (Figure 43). Add a few extra stitches at each corner to secure the mitering properly. Take care to catch only the canvas or backs of embroidery stitches as you sew. Do not allow the running stitches to show through on the right side of the finished canvas.
8. The work can now be given a gentle steaming around the edges to smooth down the folded canvas, especially at the corners.

applying the cushion strips

These patterned borders can be applied to the background of a shop-bought and -finished pillow, either down the center, as shown in Plate 3, or at either side, or top and bottom, as shown in Figure 44. They can also be used as appliqués to decorate and personalize canvas tote bags. Backed with a fabric strip, they could be used as curtain tie-backs. Instructions are given here for the method of applying a strip to a made-up pillow.

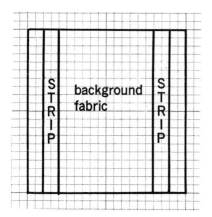

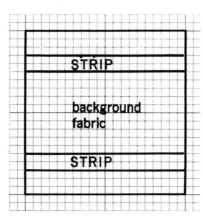

Figure 44
Positioning cushion strips

you will need

▶ A finished pillow with one of its dimensions equal to the length of the strip to be applied, that is, 14 or 16 inches in the case of borders given in the project section
You can change the length of the strips by adding or subtracting pattern repeats, provided that you work this alteration out on a graph before you begin sewing. Chapter 2 gives helpful information on how to do this and to change the yarn amounts to compensate.

▶ Regular sewing thread in a color to match the fabric to which the strip is to be applied

METHOD

1. Turn under and finish the edges of the canvas as described earlier in this chapter.
2. Mark the center of the pillow and the strip with a pin at top and bottom.
3. Align the center of the strip with the pins at the center of the pillow, and pin in place across the top and bottom (the shorter sides of the strip).
4. Pin the strip in place down the long side edges.
5. Using a small hemming stitch, sew the strip to the background fabric all the way around its edges.
6. Finish with a gentle steaming to smooth out any wrinkles in the canvas.

making a rug in "tiles"

The method for designing and working a rug, using the squares in the project section like carpet "tiles," is described in Chapter 2. The way to sew together the tiles and to finish a rug assembled in this manner is detailed here. A rug worked in one continuous piece can be finished in exactly the same way, but omitting steps 2 through 5.

you will need

- ▶ A piece of felt measuring the same as the total worked area of the rug
- ▶ A piece of nonslip backing measuring ½ inch less than the felt in each direction
  The backing looks like large-mesh leno canvas and is made of plastic. It does not fray and can be cut to the exact size required.
- ▶ Strong thread in a color to match the shade that predominates along the edges of the "tiles"

METHOD

1. Finish each square by folding under all the edges of the canvas, as described earlier in this chapter.
2. Lay all the squares, face down, on a flat surface in the order in which they are to be assembled.
3. With a sharp-pointed needle threaded with a strong sewing thread in a color that blends, join the squares together across the horizontal lines to form strips (Figure 45). Hold the squares with the right sides facing each other as you sew. Use an oversewing stitch and keep the stitches close together, always working into the holes where the last embroidery stitches were made.
4. Join the strips together along the vertical lines in the same way, so that the completed rug is assembled as shown in Figure 45. Any topstitching in embroidery yarn along the joins should be added at this point.
5. Give the rug a gentle steaming, especially along the joins, making sure that it is flat and smooth before applying the backing.
6. Place the rug, face down, on a flat surface. Trim the felt to the same size as the area of the finished rug, and pin it to the back of the rug around the edges.

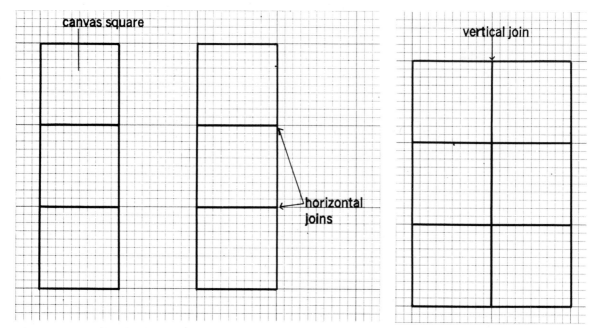

Figure 45 Assembling the rug squares

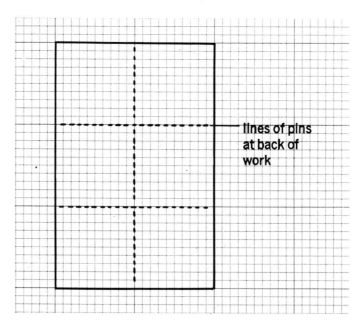

Figure 46 Pinning the backing

54

7. Oversew the felt to the rug around the outside edges, using the same strong thread previously employed to sew the squares together.
8. Lay the rug on a flat surface once more, with the felt facing up. Apply the nonslip backing, pinning it in position around the edges and in horizontal and vertical lines across the back, following the outline of the squares underneath (Figure 46).
9. Sew the backing to the felt around the outside and across the back, along the lines marked by the pins.
10. Give the rug a final light steaming on the *right* side of the work. Take care not to apply too much heat to the plastic backing, which can suffer severe damage at high temperatures.

making a wall hanging

If you are making a wall hanging using the "tile" method just described for making a rug, follow the instructions already given in this chapter for assembling the squares. Naturally, you will omit the use of a nonslip backing. Once the squares are joined together, you can finish the tiled wall hanging in exactly the same way as one worked in a continuous piece.

you will need

▶ A piece of felt measuring exactly the same as the worked area of the canvas

▶ A length of 1-inch-wide tape measuring twice the width of the finished canvas, plus 2 inches

▶ Two lengths of wooden pole, measuring not more than 1 inch in diameter and a few inches longer than the width of the finished canvas

▶ Strong thread in a color that blends with the shade of wool used at the edge of the completed canvas

▶ A length of cord for hanging the finished piece

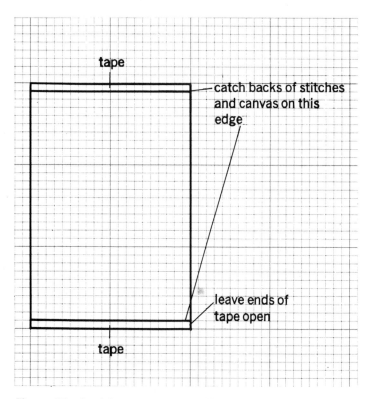

Figure 47   Applying tapes on a wall hanging

METHOD

1. Turn under and finish the edges of the canvas as described earlier in this chapter.
2. Lay the hanging, face down, on a flat surface. Trim the felt to be exactly the same size as the area of the finished sewing, and pin it to the back of the hanging, around the edges.
3. Oversew the felt to the hanging around the outside edges, using a strong thread that blends with the color at the edges of the embroidery.

4. Cut the tape in half and turn under ½ inch at each end, backstitching in place.

5. Pin the tape to the top and bottom of the hanging, as shown in Figure 47.

6. Sew the tape in place using a hemming stitch. Be sure to catch the backs of the stitches and canvas through the felt on the inside edges of the tapes (Figure 47). It is important that stitches not show through on the right side of the hanging, but at the same time you must secure the tape to the back of the canvas through the felt, so that the poles are held firmly in place when inserted. Leave the turned-under ends of the tape open, as shown in Figure 47.

7. Give a gentle steaming at this point.

8. Insert the poles between the tape and the felt, allowing a few inches to extend at either end. The wood can be painted in a color to match the design if the natural finish of the wood is not suitable. The poles can also be finished with wood stain to make them lighter or darker, then sealed with a coat of varnish. Any painting or staining of the wood should be done well in advance and the pole allowed to dry thoroughly before inserting it into the hanging.

9. The cord should now be attached to the extending ends at either side of the top pole. The length of this cord depends upon your personal taste and the positioning of the hanging. When the cord has been tied, the ends can be tucked along inside the tape at the back of the hanging. Figure 48 shows the front and back view of the completed hanging.

10. The pole at the bottom of the hanging is added to give weight that helps to keep the canvas smooth and properly stretched. You could leave it out if you prefer, mounting the entire hanging on one pole at the top.

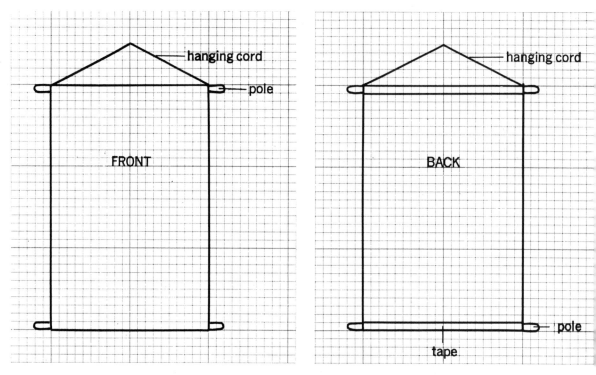

Figure 48   Front and back of completed hanging

making an eyeglasses case   The eyeglasses cases in the project section are sewn in one long strip, which is then folded in half. The size of these cases is wider than average to accommodate larger sunglasses and the bigger frames of regular glasses that are presently fashionable. If your eyeglasses are small and likely to slip out, seal the top opening with a couple of press studs.

Plate 1. Snowflake

Plate 2. Birds and Flowers

Plate 3. Snow Flower Border

Plate 4. Basket of Flowers

Plate 5. Hungarian Lady Eyeglasses Case

Plate 6. Purse in Patterned Squares

Plate 7. Squares within Squares

Plate 8. Head of a God

Plate 9. Aztec Wall Hanging

Plate 10. Indian Fabric Square

Plate 11. Mosaic Tcharka

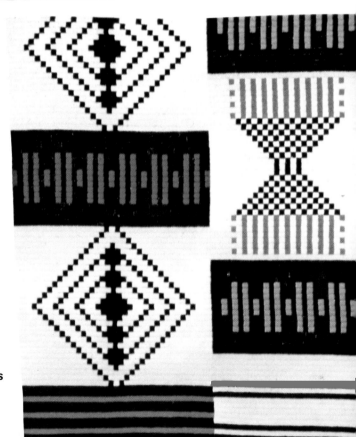

Plate 12. African Wall Hanging in Strips

Plate 13. African Wall Hanging in Diamonds

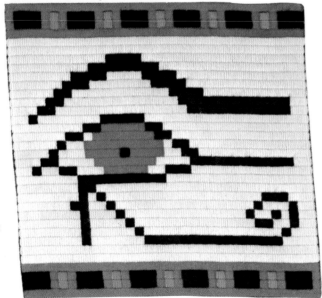

Plate 14. Eye of Ra

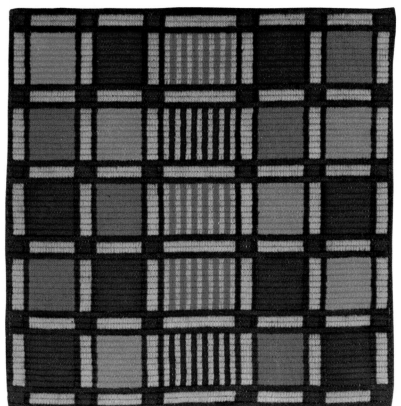

Plate 15. Egyptian Mosaic

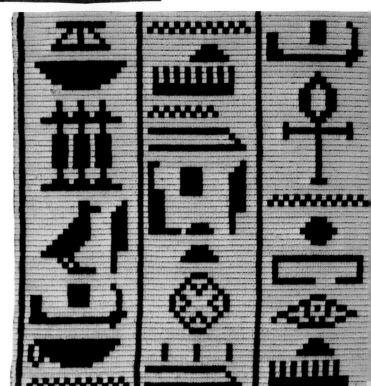

Plate 16. Egyptian Hieroglyphics

you will need

▶ A piece of felt measuring exactly the same as the area of finished embroidery

▶ Strong thread in a color to match the yarn at the edges of the work

▶ Two press studs (optional)

METHOD

1. Turn under and finish the edges of the canvas as described earlier in this chapter.
2. Place the strip of canvas, face down, on a flat surface.
3. Apply the felt to the back of the canvas and pin in place.
4. Using strong thread and a sharp-pointed needle, oversew the felt to the canvas around the edges.
5. Sew on the press studs at opposite ends of the felt backing if you are going to use them (Figure 49), making sure that they are correctly placed to snap tightly when the case is folded.
6. Fold the case in half across the middle at the point indicated for such a fold on the individual chart that accompanies each project. The right side of the canvas will then be outside, the felt inside.
7. Pin the side edges together, leaving the top edge, opposite the fold, open.
8. Oversew each side, starting at the fold and working up, matching row for row on the canvas. Use small stitches so that the matching thread blends with the wool on the canvas.
9. Give a final, gentle steaming to the seams, and apply a little more pressure than usual at the fold to create a crisp edge.

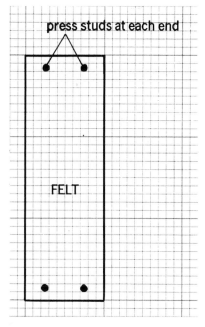

Figure 49 Position of press studs

59

making a zippered purse

Any of the rectangular canvases with a center fold, such as those shown in Figure 50, can be made into a bag with a zipper fastening. These bags can be used as eyeglasses cases, cosmetics containers, evening bags, or even document folders, according to their size.

you will need

▸ A piece of felt measuring exactly the same as the area of the finished embroidery

▸ A zipper measuring not more than 1 inch shorter than the width of the rectangular piece of embroidery

A shorter zipper can be used, but at least ½ inch must be allowed at each side for the ends of the zipper and for completing the corners. Choose a color for the zipper that blends with the finished canvas and is not too conspicuous.

▸ Strong thread to match the color of the zipper

METHOD

1. Work steps 1 through 6 as for the eyeglasses case, omitting step 5.
2. Insert the zipper at the top edge, using a backstitch to sew it in place.
3. Pin the side edges together.
4. Oversew each side, starting at the fold and working up, matching row for row on the canvas. Use small stitches so that the matching thread blends with the wool on the canvas.
5. Give a final, gentle steaming to the seams, and apply a little more pressure than usual at the fold to create a crisp edge.

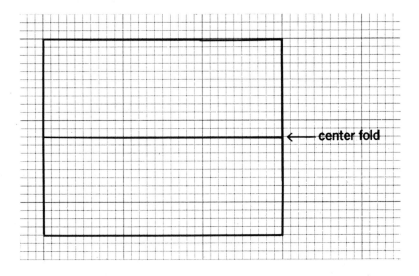

Figure 50   Rectangular canvas

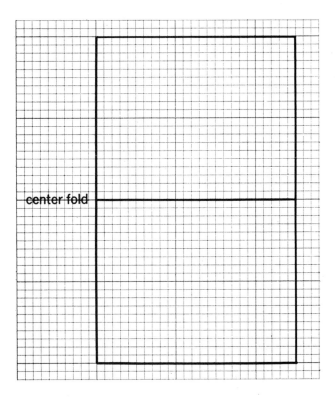

Photograph 4. Bag with felt pouch

making a flap-top bag

Any of the rectangular canvases with a center fold, such as those shown in Figure 50, can be made into this type of bag. Instead of having a zipper at the top, a false front or pouch in felt is added over which the front canvas flap folds. Photograph 4 shows the top canvas flap pushed a little to one side to reveal the felt front of the bag underneath. Eyeglasses cases can be made in this way from the smaller projects in this rectangular shape. Press studs can be used to secure the front flap to the felt pouch of the bag, or a bead and loop fastening could be added at the lower edge. These fastenings are a matter of individual taste and can be applied when the finishing of the bag is complete.

you will need

▶ A piece of felt measuring the exact width and twice the length of the finished rectangle of sewn canvas, plus ¼ inch

▶ A piece of stiff interfacing measuring ½ inch less than the width and ½ inch less than half the length of the sewn canvas

▶ Strong thread that matches the color of the felt

▶ Two press studs for fastening (optional)

METHOD

1. Turn under and finish the edges of the canvas as described earlier in this chapter.
2. Lay the canvas, face down, on a flat surface, and match the shorter side of the felt to the top edge of the canvas. Pin the felt to the canvas along the top and down the two sides. You will have a piece of felt measuring the same length as the canvas hanging from the end, as shown in Figure 51.
3. Using strong thread and a sharp-pointed needle, sew across the top edge in oversewing stitches, to join the felt and canvas together. Continue sewing down the side. Fasten off the thread at the bottom. Begin at the top again, and sew down the other side. Do not break off the thread.
4. Pin the bottom of the canvas to the felt, and attach the canvas to the felt by sewing across with a hemming stitch.
5. With the felt side of the bag facing, turn up ½ inch at the bottom and pin, as shown in Figure 52.
6. Place the stiffening fabric along the lower half of the felt (Figure 53).
7. Fold the felt up at the top of the stiffening fabric. Pin and sew in place across the horizontal line, as shown in Figure 54, using a small hemming stitch.

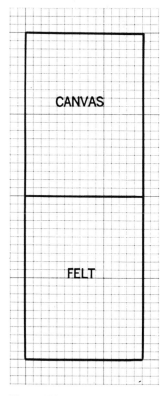

Figure 51
Canvas with felt applied

63

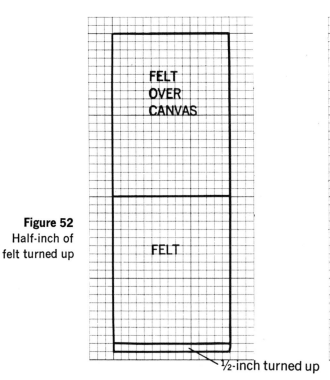

Figure 52
Half-inch of
felt turned up

Figure 53
Stiffening fabric
applied

½-inch turned up

Figure 54   Sewing felt flap in position

Figure 55   Sewing sides of felt pouch

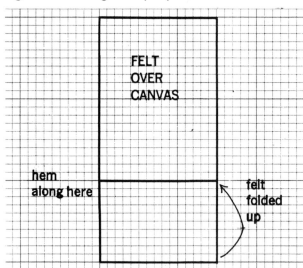

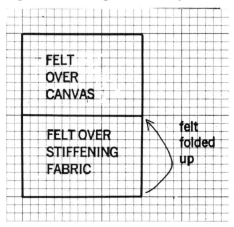

8. Fold the felt up once more. It will now reach almost halfway up the canvas. Oversew each side, starting at the bottom edge and working up, as shown in Figure 55. Use small stitches so that the matching thread blends with the felt and the wool on the canvas.

9. Fold the canvas in half along the line indicated on the individual project chart.

10. Give a final, gentle steaming to the seams, and apply a little more pressure than usual at the fold to create a crisp edge.

11. Add press studs at appropriate intervals on the canvas flap and felt pouch to fasten the bag if required.

making a document folder

you will need

▶ A piece of felt measuring exactly the same as the finished area of the embroidery

▶ A piece of stiff interfacing measuring 11¾ x 15¾ inches

▶ Strong thread in a color to match or blend with the predominant shade of the wool at the borders of the sewing

▶ Two or three press studs for fastening (optional)

METHOD

1. Turn under and finish the raw edges of the canvas as described in this chapter.

2. Lay the canvas, face down, on a flat surface, with the second fold at the top and the first fold at the bottom, as shown in Figure 56. The positions of these folds are indicated on the charts for individual projects.

3. Place the stiff interfacing at the bottom of the canvas, filling the area up to the first fold. Secure with running stitches around the edges.

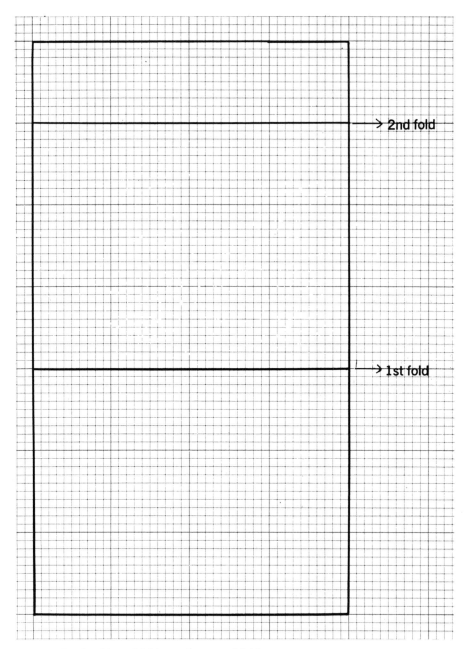

Figure 56   Position of folds on document folder

4. Place the felt on top of the canvas, and over the interfacing, pinning it in position around the edges and across the first fold line. Follow the line of the pins when sewing. Oversew the canvas to the felt at the edges, and use a running stitch across the first fold line.

5. Fold the canvas up at the first fold line. Pin the sides together. The right sides of the canvas will be facing out.

6. Oversew each side, starting at the fold and working up, matching row for row on the canvas. Use small stitches so that the matching thread blends with the wool on the canvas.

7. Fold down on the second fold line to make an overlapping flap of canvas. Sew press studs onto this flap and in corresponding places on the canvas below, if you have chosen to have a fastening.

8. Give a final, gentle steaming to the seams, and apply a little more pressure than usual at the folds to create crisp edges.

making a tote bag

You may use any of the squares or rectangles given in the project section, provided that they are of a suitable size. You will need to make two canvas sides for this particular method of assembling a tote bag.

you will need

▶ Two squares or rectangles worked in canvas
You need not use the same design for each side of the bag, provided that the sides are equal in size.

▶ A piece of felt measuring the exact width of the top and twice the length of the side of the bag

▶ Two pieces of cord or strong tape suitable for handles, each measuring 10 inches

▶ Strong thread to blend with the color predominating at the edges of the worked canvas

METHOD

1. Join the canvases together across a horizontal line, as shown in Figure 57. Keep the canvases' right sides together when sewing, and machine stitch into the holes of the canvas where the last embroidery stitches were worked. If the canvases are made into a design that has a top and bottom to it, make sure that the lower part of each design is at the joining line. In this

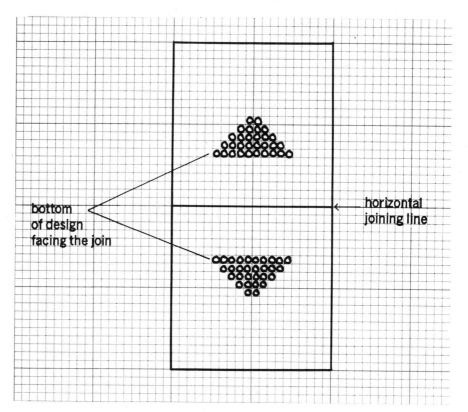

Figure 57 Two halves of tote bag joined at center seam

68

way the pattern will be the correct way up when the bag is finished.

2. Trim the canvas to within 1 inch of the sewing along the join. Open out the seam so that the border of canvas lies flat on either side of the sewing. Steam this seam open and flat.

3. Turn under and finish the raw edges of the canvas (now in one piece) as described earlier in this chapter.

4. Apply the cords, one at each end of the canvas, on the wrong side, as shown in Figure 58. Sew the cords in place with an overlap of 2 inches at each end. Make certain that the sewing catches the canvas but does not go through to show on the right side of the canvas.

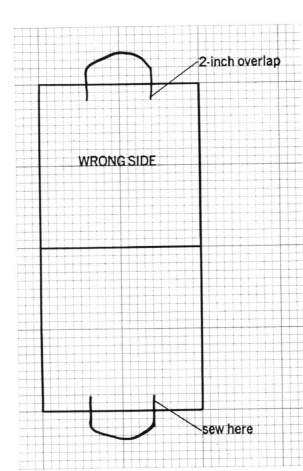

2-inch overlap

WRONG SIDE

sew here

Figure 58
Position of cord handles

5. Place the canvas, face down, on a flat surface. Apply the felt to the canvas and pin in place around the edges and across the joining line.
6. Oversew the canvas to the felt around the edges, sewing across the cords. Work a running stitch across the joining line.
7. Fold the bag in half at the joining line and pin the side seams together. The right sides of the bag will be facing out.
8. Oversew each side, starting at the fold and working up, matching row for row on the canvas. Use small stitches so that the matching thread blends with the wool on the canvas.
9. Give a final, gentle steaming to the seams, and apply a little more pressure than usual at the fold to create a crisp edge.

THE PROJECTS

Please read the following notes carefully before embarking on any of the projects.

I have graded the designs in this section according to the standard of skill required to work the canvas. The "star" system works as follows:

* means that the design is suitable for the absolute beginner.

** means that the design requires a medium range of ability and is suitable for the person who has had some prior experience with straight-stitch work.

*** indicates that the design is suitable for the very experienced worker only.

It is possible to chart a course for yourself through the three-star system of this book, increasing the difficulty and challenge of the projects you choose, as you build confidence in the lower ratings.

Use all three strands of Persian needlepoint wool unless otherwise instructed on a specific design. Some of the projects are worked on a finer canvas with two strands of Persian yarn. To avoid wasting the extra strand on each length of yarn you cut, keep all threads the same size. This is easily achieved by using the "wrap-around-the-ruler" method to cut the yarn, as shown in Figure 2, page 9.

Peel off the extra strand of yarn on each length by starting in the center, as illustrated in Figure 59. When you have done this on two lengths of yarn, put the remaining two strands side by side and thread the needle with them. Continue working in the usual way.

All work is in simple upright Gobelin stitch unless otherwise indicated on a specific project.

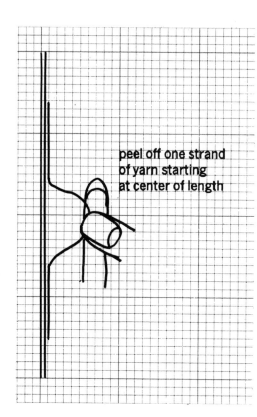

peel off one strand of yarn starting at center of length

Figure 59
Peeling off one strand of yarn

Snow Crystals

scandinavian designs

snow crystals ✳

Snow plays an important part in traditional Scandinavian crafts. Strictly speaking, snow crystals are all hexagonal (six-sided), but multiples of four are much easier to cope with in decorative design. Thus many of the snow motifs, like this one, have eight sides or points.

FINISHED SIZE   Approx. 16 x 16 inches

you need

▶ Persian needlepoint wool in 10-yard skeins:

Beige	12	(120 yards)
Medium brown	1	(10 yards)
Dark brown	4	(40 yards)
Pale orange	2	(20 yards)

▶ A piece of ten-mesh-to-one-inch mono canvas measuring 20 x 20 inches

▶ A number 18 tapestry needle

METHOD

1. The entire design is worked over four mesh of the canvas.
2. Find the center of the canvas as shown in Chapter 2.
3. Find the center square of the chart as shown in Chapter 2.
4. Begin working at center square, following chart shown in Figure 60, and sewing from right to left toward left edge. Return to center square and complete center row to right edge. Continue working in rows until entire chart is completed.

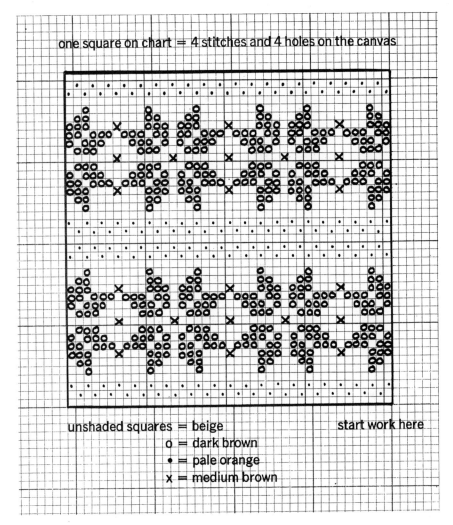

Figure 60 Snow Crystals

snowflake **
(Plate 1)

Worked in the shimmering white and blues of sunlit ice, this magnificent snowflake most beautifully illustrates the central core of the Scandinavian tradition of decorating in "snow" shapes.

FINISHED SIZE   Approx. 16 x 16 inches

you need

▶ Persian needlepoint wool in 10 yard skeins:

White	11	(110 yards)
Dark blue	6	(60 yards)
Medium blue	4	(40 yards)
Light blue	2	(20 yards)

▶ A piece of ten-mesh-to-one-inch mono canvas measuring 20 x 20 inches

▶ A number 18 tapestry needle

METHOD

1. The entire design is worked over four mesh of the canvas.
2. Find the center of the canvas as shown in Chapter 2.
3. Find the center square of the chart as shown in Chapter 2.
4. Begin working at center square, following chart shown in Figure 61, and sewing from right to left toward left edge. Return to center square and complete center row to right edge. Continue working in rows until entire chart is completed.

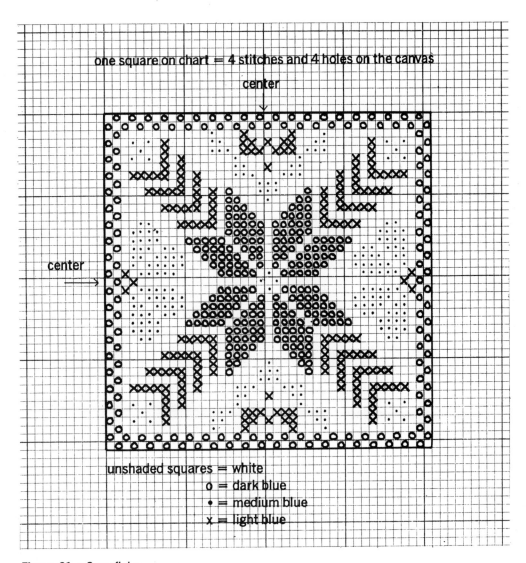

Figure 61 Snowflake

Snow Flowers

snow flowers **

Stylized geometric floral motifs, such as the one used in this design, are a recurring feature of Scandinavian decorative crafts. In the clean lines of their geometry, the flowers seem to state their close resemblance to snow crystals.

FINISHED SIZE   Approx. 14 x 14 inches

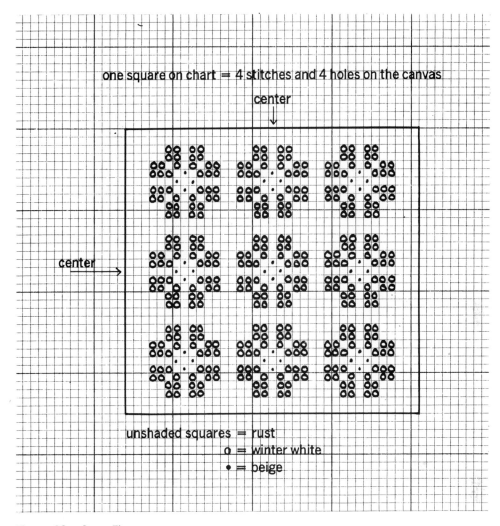

one square on chart = 4 stitches and 4 holes on the canvas

center

center

unshaded squares = rust
o = winter white
• = beige

Figure 62 Snow Flowers

you need

▸ Persian needlepoint wool in 10-yard skeins:

Rust	7	(70 yards)
Winter white	2	(20 yards)
Beige	1	(10 yards)

▸ A piece of ten-mesh-to-one-inch mono canvas measuring 18 x 18 inches

▸ A number 18 tapestry needle

79

METHOD

1. The entire design is worked over four mesh of the canvas.
2. Find the center of the canvas as shown in Chapter 2.
3. Find the center square of the chart as shown in Chapter 2.
4. Begin working at center square, following chart shown in Figure 62, and sewing from right to left, to left edge. Return to center square and complete center row to right side. Continue working in rows until entire chart is completed.

bands of flowers **

A striking rug could be made by alternating squares of this pretty pattern as shown in Figure 27. Please refer to Chapter 3 for full instructions for making tiled rugs. If you want to make a wall hanging, you can make the squares in Persian yarn as indicated in the instructions, and then sew them together in the same pattern as for the rug.

FINISHED SIZE   Approx. 14 x 14 inches

you need

▶ Persian needlepoint wool in 10-yard skeins:

Dark brown	10	(100 yards)
Winter white	3	(30 yards)
Copper	2	(20 yards)

▶ A piece of ten-mesh-to-one-inch mono canvas measuring 18 x 18 inches
▶ A number 18 tapestry needle

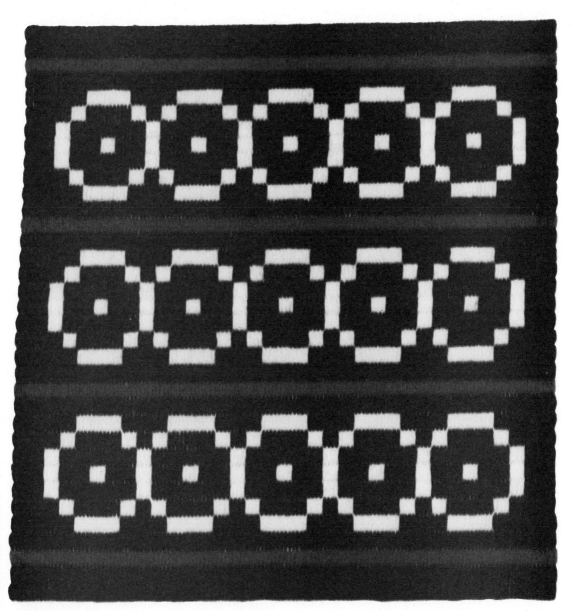

Bands of Flowers

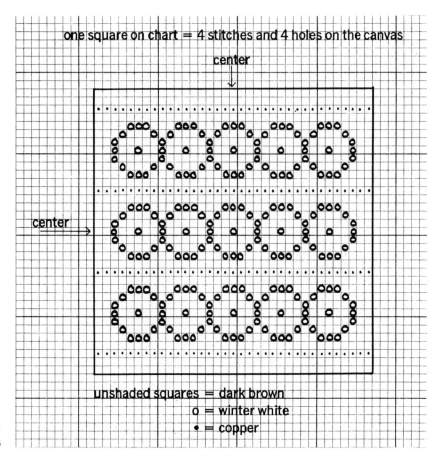

one square on chart = 4 stitches and 4 holes on the canvas

center

center

unshaded squares = dark brown
o = winter white
• = copper

Figure 63
Bands of Flowers

METHOD

1. The entire design is worked over four mesh of the canvas.
2. Find the center of the canvas as shown in Chapter 3.
3. Begin working at center square, following chart shown in Figure 63, and sewing from right to left, to left edge. Return to center square and complete center row to right edge. Continue working in rows until entire chart is completed.

birds and flowers **
(Plate 2)

This design incorporates some of the most popular and decorative Scandinavian motifs: the heart, the bird, and, of course, flowers. Mounted or framed, it would make an attractive picture.

FINISHED SIZE   Approx. 14 x 14 inches

you need

▶ Persian needlepoint wool in 10-yard skeins:

Beige	6	(60 yards)
Copper	4	(40 yards)
Red	2	(20 yards)
Orange	2	(20 yards)
Cream	2	(20 yards)
Brown	1	(10 yards)
Dark green	1	(10 yards)
Light orange	1	(10 yards)

▶ A piece of ten-mesh-to-one-inch mono canvas measuring 18 x 18 inches
▶ A number 18 tapestry needle

METHOD

1. The entire design is worked over four mesh of the canvas.
2. Start in lower right corner, at a point 2 inches up from bottom and in from side edge.
3. Following the chart shown in Figure 64, begin work where indicated by the arrow. Work in rows across, until entire chart is completed.

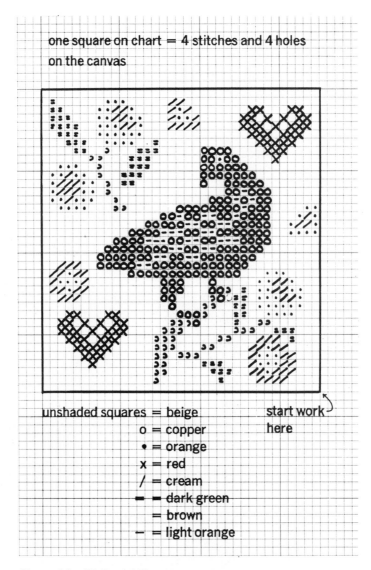

one square on chart = 4 stitches and 4 holes on the canvas

unshaded squares = beige
o = copper
• = orange
x = red
/ = cream
▬ ▬ = dark green
= brown
— = light orange

start work here

Figure 64 Birds and Flowers

purse in a heart motif ✳✳✳

This small purse could be made into an eyeglasses case or a cosmetics bag. There are any number of uses to which a small container like this can be put in a woman's handbag. A selection of methods for finishing rectangular shapes like this is given in Chapter 3.

FINISHED SIZE   Approx. 7 x 8 inches (7 x 4 inches when folded)

you need

▸ Persian needlepoint wool in 10-yard skeins:

Black	3	(30 yards)
White	2	(20 yards)
Red	3	(30 yards)

▸ A piece of eighteen-mesh-to-one-inch mono canvas measuring 9 x 10 inches

▸ A number 22 tapestry needle

Purse in a Heart Motif

SPECIAL NOTE   The entire design is worked with only *two* strands of the Persian yarn instead of the usual three.

METHOD

1. The entire design is worked over four mesh of the canvas.
2. Start in lower right corner, at a point 1 inch up from bottom and in from side edge.
3. Following the chart shown in Figure 65, begin work where indicated by the arrow. Work in rows across, until entire chart is completed.

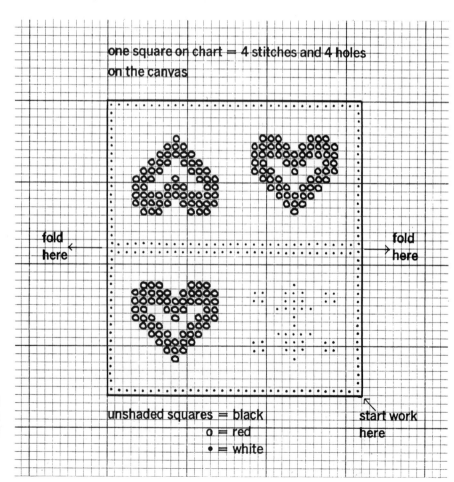

one square on chart = 4 stitches and 4 holes on the canvas

fold here

fold here

Figure 65
Purse in Heart
Motif

unshaded squares = black
o = red
• = white

start work here

cushion strips

There follows a selection of border designs that can be used, singly or in twos, to brighten up a plain fabric pillow. Instructions on how to apply the strips to a background are given in Chapter 3.

You can also use these borders to add width to a design of your own, as discussed in Chapter 2. Repeat the borders side by side across a canvas to create a striped effect in any size you require. Figures 66 and 67 offer two methods of using the strips to make a new design.

The strips are marked as "difficult" because they are worked on a very fine canvas.

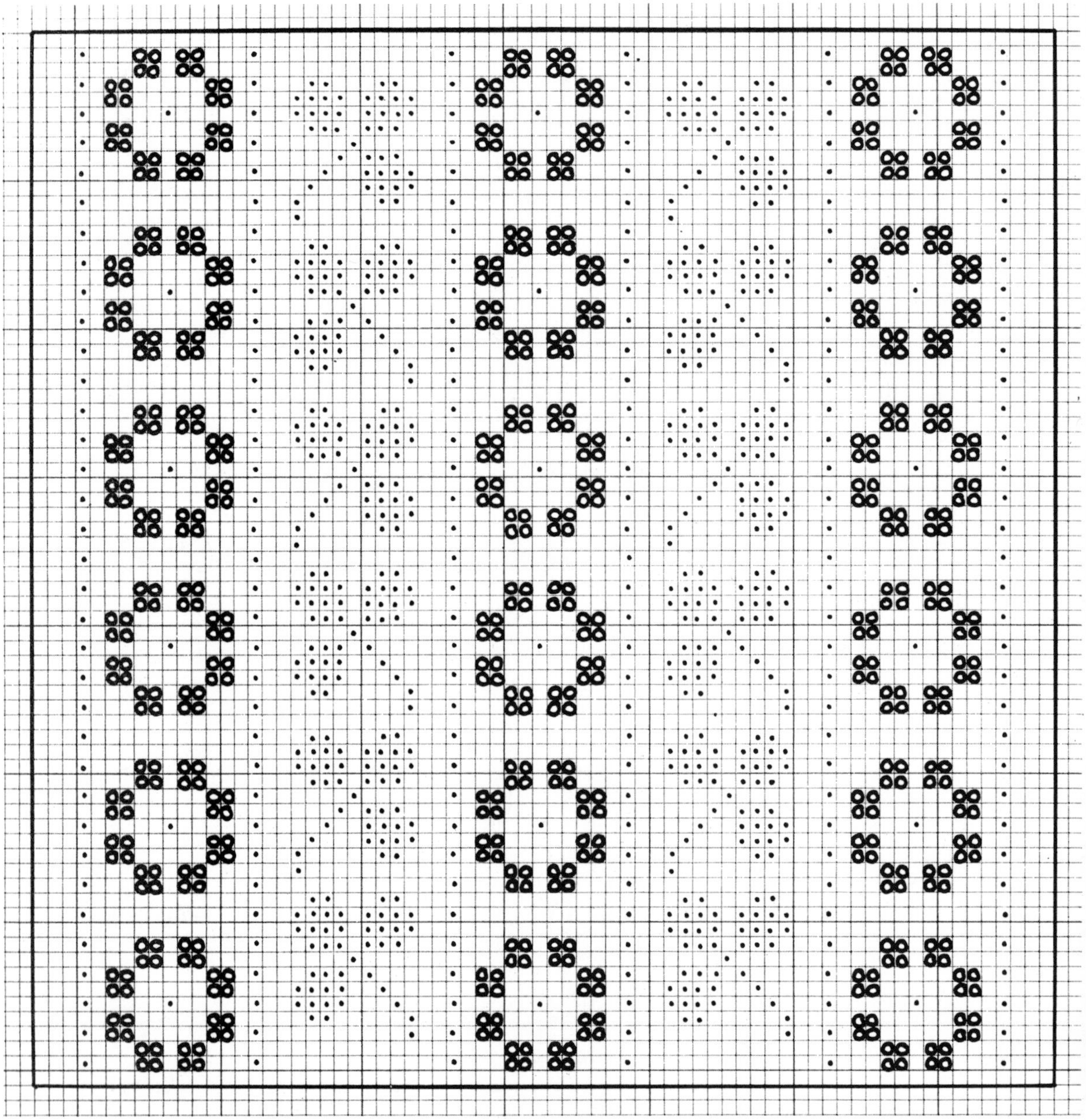

Figure 66 Borders side by side—bands of pattern can be worked vertically as shown, or horizontally, by simply turning the chart on its side

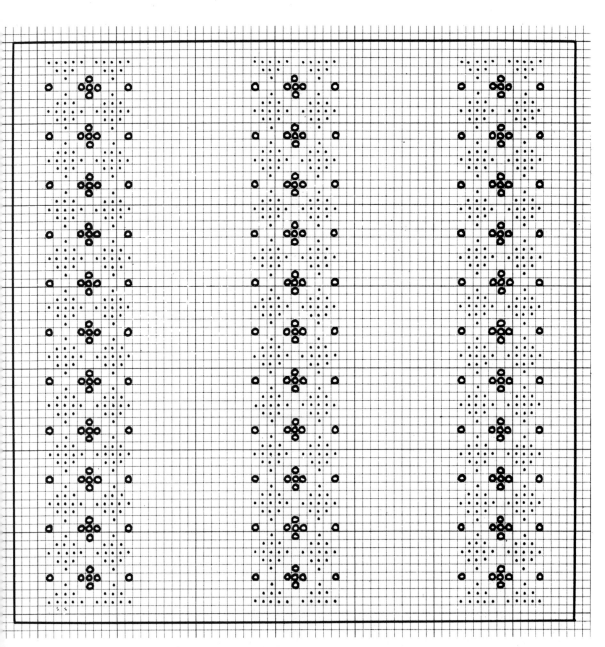

Figure 67 Borders alternating with plain strips—bands of pattern can be worked vertically as shown, or horizontally, by simply turning the chart on its side

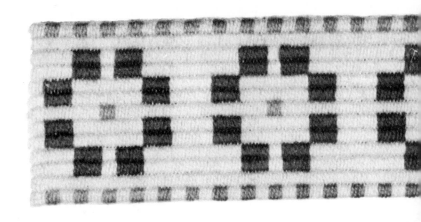

rose border ✳✳✳

FINISHED SIZE   Approx. 16 x 3 inches

you need

▶ Persian needlepoint wool in 10-yard skeins:

Rose red	2	(20 yards)
Rose pink	1	(10 yards)
Off-white	3	(30 yards)

▶ A piece of eighteen-mesh-to-one-inch mono canvas measuring 18 x 5 inches

▶ A number 22 tapestry needle

SPECIAL NOTE   The entire design is worked with only *two* strands of the Persian yarn instead of the usual three.

METHOD

1. The entire design is worked over four mesh of the canvas.
2. Start in lower right corner, at a point 1 inch up from bottom and in from side edge.
3. Following the chart shown in Figure 68, begin work where indicated by the arrow. Work in rows across, until entire chart is completed.

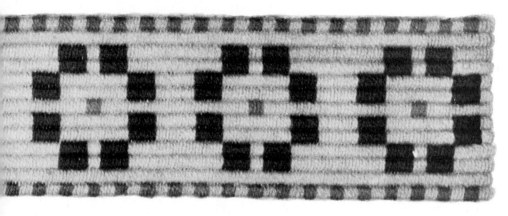

Rose Border

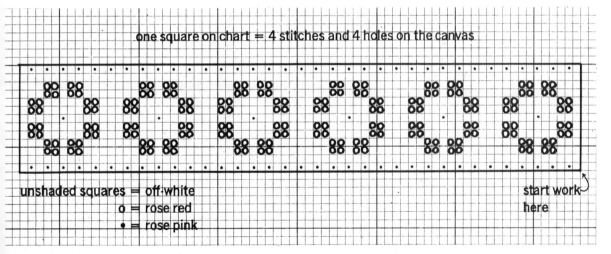

one square on chart = 4 stitches and 4 holes on the canvas

unshaded squares = off-white
o = rose red
• = rose pink

start work here

Figure 68   Rose Border

snow flower border ✳✳✳
(Plate 3)

FINISHED SIZE   Approx. 16 x 3 inches

you need

▸ Persian needlepoint wool in 10-yard skeins:

Brown	3	(30 yards)
Cream	2	(20 yards)
Medium brown	2	(20 yards)

▸ A piece of eighteen-mesh-to-one-inch mono canvas measuring 18 x 5 inches

▸ A number 22 tapestry needle

SPECIAL NOTE   The entire design is worked with only *two* strands of the Persian yarn instead of the usual three.

METHOD

1. The entire design is worked over four mesh of the canvas.
2. Start in lower right corner, at a point 1 inch up from bottom and in from side edge.
3. Following the chart shown in Figure 69, begin work where indicated by the arrow. Work in rows across, until entire chart is completed.

Figure 69   Snow Flower Border

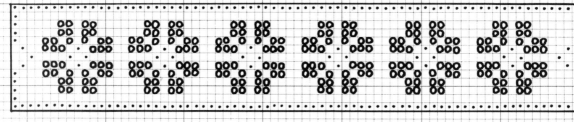

one square on chart = 4 stitches and 4 holes on the canvas

unshaded squares = brown
o = cream
• = medium brown

start work here

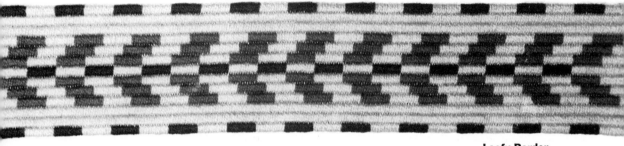

Leafy Border

leafy border ***

FINISHED SIZE   Approx. 16 x 3 inches

you need

- Persian needlepoint wool in 10-yard skeins:

Spring green	3	(30 yards)
Dark gold	2	(20 yards)
Dark green	1	(10 yards)

- A piece of eighteen-mesh-to-one-inch mono canvas measuring 18 x 5 inches
- A number 22 tapestry needle

SPECIAL NOTE   The entire design is worked with only *two* strands of the Persian yarn instead of the usual three.

METHOD

1. The entire design is worked over four mesh of the canvas.

2. Start in lower right corner, at a point 1 inch up from bottom and in from side edge.
3. Following the chart shown in Figure 70, begin work where indicated by the arrow. Work in rows across, until entire chart is completed.

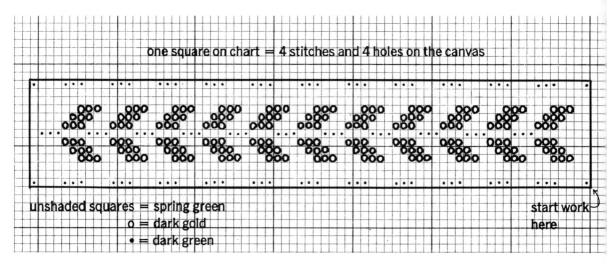

one square on chart = 4 stitches and 4 holes on the canvas

unshaded squares = spring green
o = dark gold
• = dark green

start work here

Figure 70 Leafy Border

clover leaf border ✳✳✳

FINISHED SIZE   Approx. 16 x 3 inches

you need

▸ Persian needlepoint wool in 10-yard skeins:

Light green	3	(30 yards)
Dark green	2	(20 yards)

▸ A piece of eighteen-mesh-to-one-inch mono canvas measuring 18 x 5 inches
▸ A number 22 tapestry needle

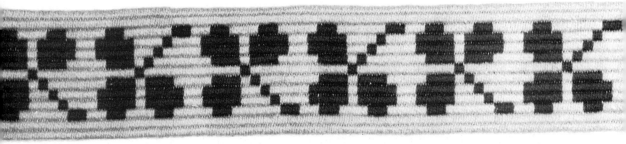

Clover Leaf Border

SPECIAL NOTE The entire design is worked with only *two* strands of the Persian yarn instead of the usual three.

METHOD

1. The entire design is worked over four mesh of the canvas.
2. Start in lower right corner, at a point 1 inch up from bottom and in from side edge.
3. Following the chart shown in Figure 71, begin work where indicated by the arrow. Work in rows across, until entire chart is completed.

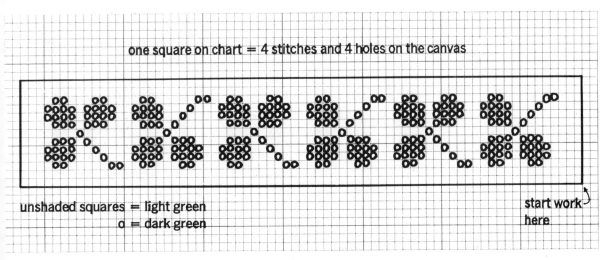

one square on chart = 4 stitches and 4 holes on the canvas

unshaded squares = light green
o = dark green

start work
here

Figure 71 Clover Leaf Border

Squared Medallions

persian and eastern european designs

squared medallions *

A simple geometric pattern such as one might find along the border of any number of carpets, this design has been re-arranged to create a square. Clearly contrasting colors would best show up the different shapes within shapes that make the pattern look complicated, although it is superbly simple to sew.

FINISHED SIZE   Approx. 16 x 16 inches

you need

▸ Persian needlepoint wool in 10-yard skeins:

Black	10	(100 yards)
Red	6	(60 yards)
White	3	(30 yards)

▸ A piece of ten-mesh-to-one-inch mono canvas measuring 20 x 20 inches

▸ A number 18 tapestry needle

METHOD

1. The entire design is worked over four mesh of the canvas.
2. Start in lower right corner, at a point 2 inches up from bottom and in from side edge.
3. Following the chart shown in Figure 72, begin work where indicated by the arrow. Work in rows across, until entire chart is completed.

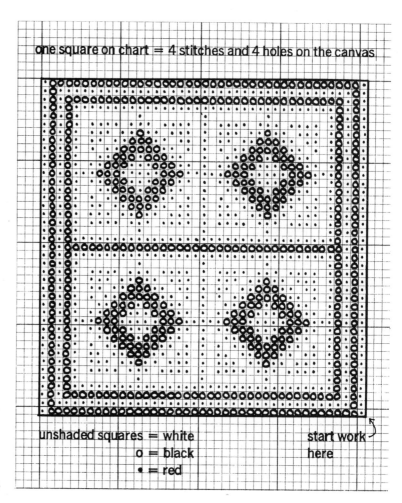

Figure 72   Squared Medallions

98

eastern carpet **

In this design a central rose motif, reminiscent of many similar floral shapes in Scandinavian decoration, is encased in border upon border, creating the effect of a carpet in miniature. The pattern would look effective picked out in subtle blends of the same shade, or in the sharply contrasting colors that I chose for my own sample.

FINISHED SIZE   Approx. 16 x 16 inches

you need

▶ Persian needlepoint wool in 10-yard skeins:

Black	9	(90 yards)
White	6	(60 yards)
Red	5	(50 yards)

▶ A piece of ten-mesh-to-one-inch mono canvas measuring 20 x 20 inches

▶ A number 18 tapestry needle

METHOD

1. The entire design is worked over four mesh of the canvas.
2. Find the center of the canvas as shown in Chapter 2.
3. Find the center square of the chart as shown in Chapter 2.
4. Begin working at center square, following chart shown in Figure 73, and sewing from right to left, toward left edge. Return to center square and complete center row to right side. Continue working in rows until entire chart is completed.

Eastern Carpet

100

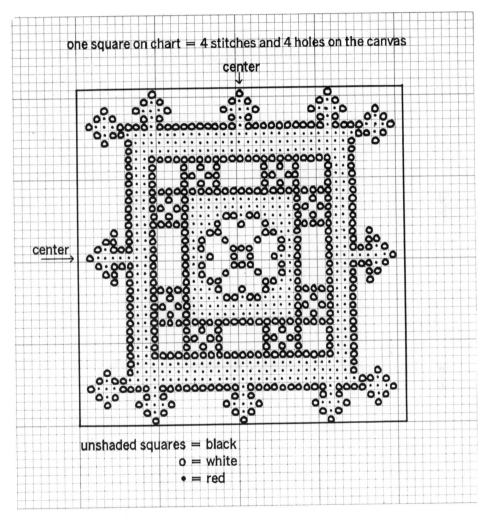

one square on chart = 4 stitches and 4 holes on the canvas

center

center

unshaded squares = black
o = white
• = red

Figure 73 Eastern Carpet

Star of the East

star of the east **

The star in the center of this design is reminiscent of the many snowflake patterns one can find in Scandinavian decorative art. All these motifs probably have a common ancestry, originating in the farthest reaches of China and brought into Europe centuries ago by the invading Mongol hordes. The treatment of the motif is different in this design, where we find the "snowflake" enclosed in a neat octagonal medallion, which itself is bounded by a square border. This application of shape upon shape is typical of the complexity of Eastern decoration. Fortunately, that does not make the design difficult to sew.

FINISHED SIZE   Approx. 16 x 16 inches

you need

▶ Persian needlepoint wool in 10-yard skeins:

Copper	11	(110 yards)
Beige	3	(30 yards)
Chocolate	3	(30 yards)

▶ A piece of ten-mesh-to-one-inch mono canvas measuring 20 x 20 inches

▶ A number 18 tapestry needle

METHOD

1. The entire design is worked over four mesh of the canvas.
2. Find the center of the canvas as shown in Chapter 2.
3. Find the center square of the chart as shown in Chapter 2.
4. Begin working at center square, following chart shown in Figure 74, and sewing from right to left, toward left edge. Return to center square and complete center row to right edge. Continue working in rows until entire chart is completed.

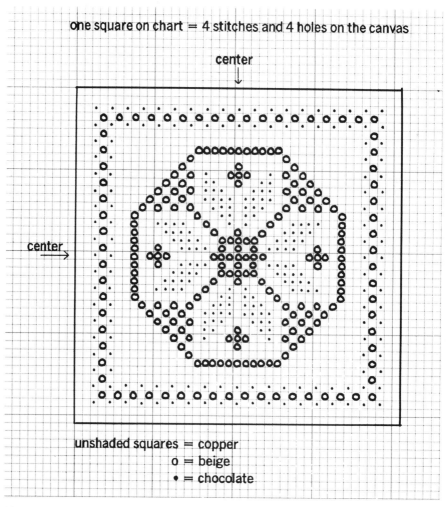

Figure 74 Star of the East

motif in scrolls ❖❖

Small squares and diamonds are here interwoven by some delicate scrolled work to form a large central motif. The complexities of the medallion are encased by a simple border pattern, to give this design its characteristic Eastern look.

FINISHED SIZE   Approx. 16 x 16 inches

you need

▶ Persian needlepoint wool in 10-yard skeins:

Orange	11	(110 yards)
Winter white	6	(60 yards)
Rust	2	(20 yards)

▶ A piece of ten-mesh-to-one-inch mono canvas measuring 20 x 20 inches

▶ A number 18 tapestry needle

METHOD

1. The entire design is worked over four mesh of the canvas.
2. Find the center of the canvas as shown in Chapter 2.
3. Find the center square of the chart as shown in Chapter 2.
4. Begin working at center square, following chart shown in Figure 75, and sewing from right to left, toward left edge. Return to center square and complete center row to right edge. Continue working in rows until entire chart is completed.

Motif in Scrolls

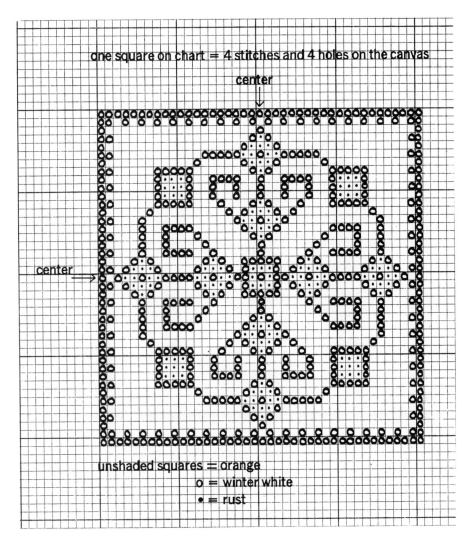

Figure 75 Motif in Scrolls

basket of flowers ✳✳✳
(Plate 4)

This charming floral bouquet was inspired by a piece of Hungarian embroidery and keeps close to tradition with its black background and brilliant colors as a contrast. This combination is particularly successful in a flower design where the mood is so cheerful and bright. The canvas would be ideal for making into a picture.

FINISHED SIZE   Approx. 14 x 14 inches

you need

▸ Persian needlepoint wool in 10-yard skeins:

Black	7	(70 yards)
Red	4	(40 yards)
Royal blue	2	(20 yards)
Bright gold	4	(40 yards)
Magenta	1	(10 yards)
Medium blue	2	(20 yards)
Spring green	1	(10 yards)

▸ A piece of ten-mesh-to-one-inch mono canvas measuring 18 x 18 inches
▸ A number 18 tapestry needle

METHOD

1. The entire design is worked over four mesh of the canvas.
2. Start in lower right corner at a point 2 inches up from bottom and in from side edge.
3. Following the chart shown in Figure 76, begin work where indicated by the arrow. Work in rows across, until entire chart is completed.

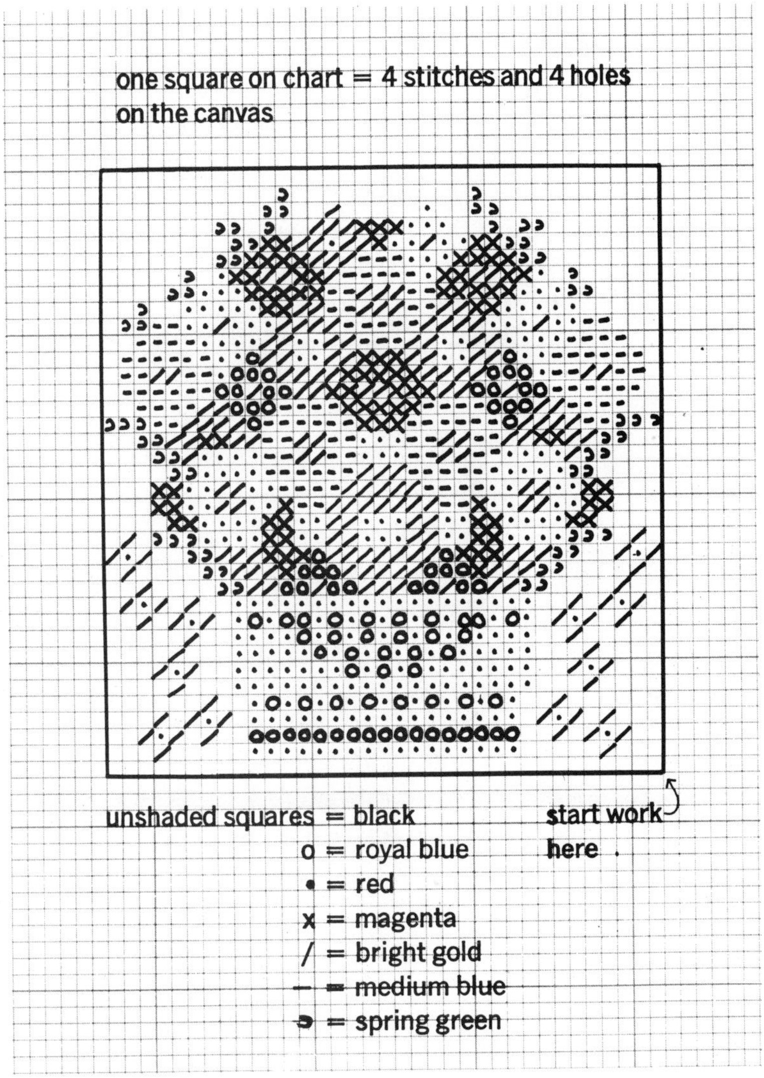
one square on chart = 4 stitches and 4 holes on the canvas
unshaded squares = black
o = royal blue
• = red
x = magenta
/ = bright gold
— = medium blue
ɔ = spring green
start work here

Figure 76 Basket of Flowers

hungarian lady eyeglasses case ✳✳✳
(Plate 5)

This eyeglasses case is worked in one continuous strip and then folded across the center, as shown on the chart. The lady appears upside down on one half of the design, so that she will, in fact, be the correct way up when the canvas is folded. For full instructions on how to finish the case, please turn to Chapter 3.

FINISHED SIZE   Approx. 14 x 3 inches

you need

> Persian needlepoint wool in 10-yard skeins:

Orange	1	(10 yards)
Turquoise	1	(10 yards)
Green	1	(10 yards)
Black	5	(50 yards)

> A piece of eighteen-mesh-to-one-inch mono canvas measuring 16 x 6 inches
> A number 22 tapestry needle

SPECIAL NOTE   The entire design is worked with only *two* strands of the Persian yarn instead of the usual 3.

METHOD

1. The entire design is worked over four mesh of the canvas.
2. Start in lower right corner, at a point 1 inch up from bottom and in from side edge.
3. Following the chart shown in Figure 77, begin work where indicated by the arrow. Work in rows across, until entire chart is completed.

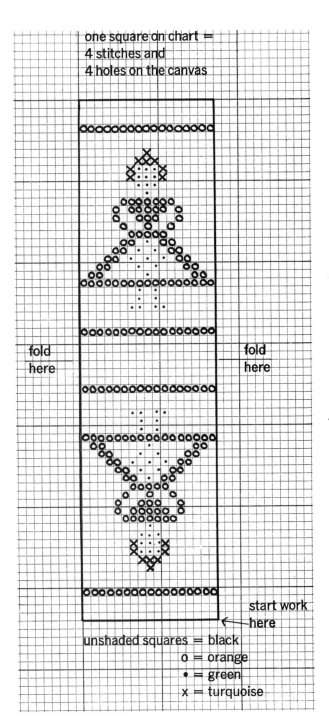

one square on chart =
4 stitches and
4 holes on the canvas

fold
here

fold
here

start work
here

unshaded squares = black
o = orange
• = green
x = turquoise

Figure 77
Hungarian Lady
Eyeglasses Case

111

american patchwork designs

patchwork checkers *

For the sake of convenience in illustrating the design, I have chosen to work the patches in four colors. However, you could use many more than that and, in the thrifty tradition of fabric patchwork, use this project to finish up all the leftover yarn in your sewing basket.

FINISHED SIZE   Approx. 16 x 16 inches

you need

▶ Persian needlepoint wool in 10-yard skeins:
Light blue	4	(40 yards)
Navy blue	6	(60 yards)
White	6	(60 yards)
Medium blue	5	(50 yards)

▶ A piece of ten-mesh-to-one-inch mono canvas measuring 20 x 20 inches

▶ A number 18 tapestry needle

Patchwork Checkers

METHOD

1. The entire design is worked over four mesh of the canvas.
2. Start in lower right corner, at a point 2 inches up from bottom and in from side edge.
3. Following the chart shown in Figure 78, begin work where indicated by the arrow. Work in rows across, until entire chart is completed.

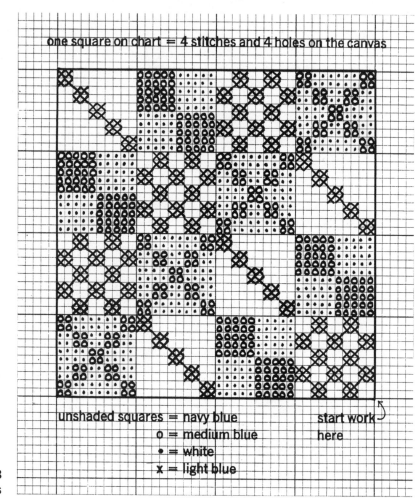

one square on chart = 4 stitches and 4 holes on the canvas

unshaded squares = navy blue
o = medium blue
• = white
x = light blue

start work here

Figure 78
Patchwork Checkers

114

Purse in Striped Patches

purse in striped patches *

This canvas, when completed, is folded across the center line as indicated on the chart. A zipper is then inserted at the top to make a useful evening or daytime bag. Full instructions on finishing the purse appear in Chapter 3.

FINISHED SIZE   Approx. 10 x 12 inches (10 x 6 inches when folded)

you need

▶ Persian needlepoint wool in 10-yard skeins:

Dark green	3	(30 yards)
Emerald green	3	(30 yards)
Medium green	3	(30 yards)
Light green	3	(30 yards)

▶ A piece of ten-mesh-to-one-inch mono canvas measuring 12 x 14 inches

▶ A number 18 tapestry needle

METHOD

1. The entire design is worked over four mesh of the canvas.
2. Start in lower right corner, at a point 1 inch up from bottom and in from side edge.
3. Following the chart shown in Figure 79, begin work where indicated by the arrow. Work in rows across, until entire chart is completed.

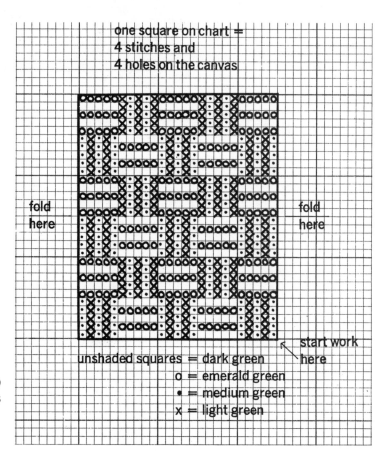

Figure 79
Purse in Striped Patches

Purse in Log Cabin Patchwork

purse in log cabin patchwork *

The finished rectangle is folded at the point shown on the chart and can be made into a useful small bag by inserting a zipper at the top. Full finishing instructions are given in Chapter 3.

FINISHED SIZE   Approx. 10 x 12 inches (10 x 6 inches when folded)

you need

▸ Persian needlepoint wool in 10-yard skeins:

White	3	(30 yards)
Medium blue	2	(20 yards)
Navy blue	3	(30 yards)
Light blue	2	(20 yards)

▶ A piece of ten-mesh-to-one-inch mono canvas measuring 12 x 14 inches

▶ A number 18 tapestry needle

METHOD

1. The entire design is worked over four mesh of the canvas.
2. Start in lower right corner, at a point 1 inch up from bottom and in from side edge.
3. Following the chart shown in Figure 80, begin work where indicated by the arrow. Work in rows across, until entire chart is completed.

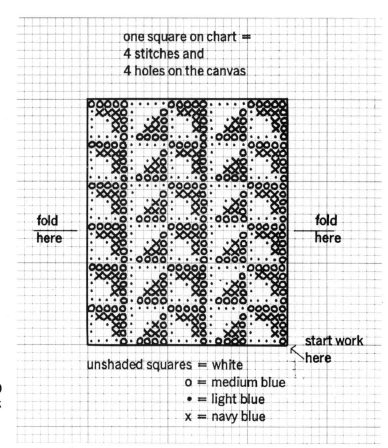

one square on chart =
4 stitches and
4 holes on the canvas

fold here

fold here

start work here

unshaded squares = white
o = medium blue
• = light blue
x = navy blue

Figure 80
Purse in Log Cabin Patchwork

document folder in patterned squares ✽

Although this is a large project for an absolute beginner, it is so easy to sew that I am able to recommend it. Each of the twenty-eight squares is different and fun to make. Use the four colors suggested for the design, or experiment with a lot more color, finishing up scraps of yarn left over from other projects. The finished canvas is folded in two places, as shown on the chart, to make an overlapping flap. Full finishing instructions appear in Chapter 3.

FINISHED SIZE   Approx. 16 x 28 inches (16 x 12 inches when folded)

you need

▸ Persian needlepoint wool in 10-yard skeins:

Dark gray	9	(90 yards)
Winter white	9	(90 yards)
Medium gray	9	(90 yards)
Light gray	9	(90 yards)

▸ A piece of ten-mesh-to-one-inch mono canvas measuring 20 x 32 inches
▸ A number 18 tapestry needle

METHOD

1. The entire design is worked over four mesh of the canvas.
2. Start in lower right corner, at a point 2 inches up from bottom and in from side edge.
3. Following the chart shown in Figure 81, begin work where indicated by the arrow. Work in rows across, until entire chart is completed.

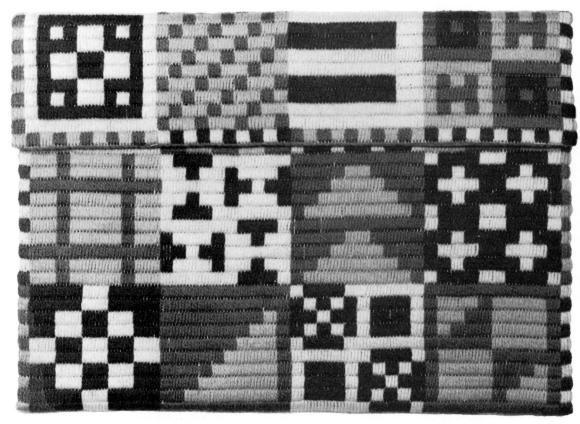

Document Folder in Patterned Squares

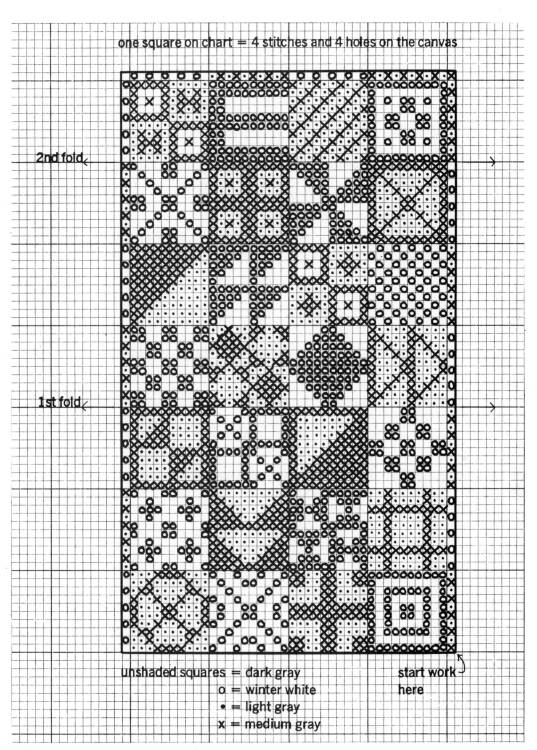

one square on chart = 4 stitches and 4 holes on the canvas

2nd fold

1st fold

unshaded squares = dark gray   start work here

o = winter white
• = light gray
x = medium gray

Figure 81   Document Folder in Patterned Squares

121

purse in patterned squares **
(Plate 6)

This design is worked over two mesh of the canvas. Useful advice on how to work this stitch is given in Chapter 2. In order to finish the canvas as a bag, please turn to Chapter 3 for instructions. The design is folded along the center line when finished, as shown on the chart.

FINISHED SIZE   Approx. 9½ x 12½ inches (9½ x 6¼ inches when folded)

you need

▶ Persian needlepoint wool in 10-yard skeins:

Medium blue	4	(40 yards)
Navy blue	5	(50 yards)
White	4	(40 yards)

▶ A piece of ten-mesh-to-one-inch mono canvas measuring 12 x 15 inches

▶ A number 18 tapestry needle

METHOD

1. The entire design is worked over two mesh of the canvas.
2. Start in lower right corner, at a point 1 inch up from bottom and in from side edge.
3. Following the chart shown in Figure 82, begin work where indicated by the arrow. Work in rows across, until entire chart is completed.

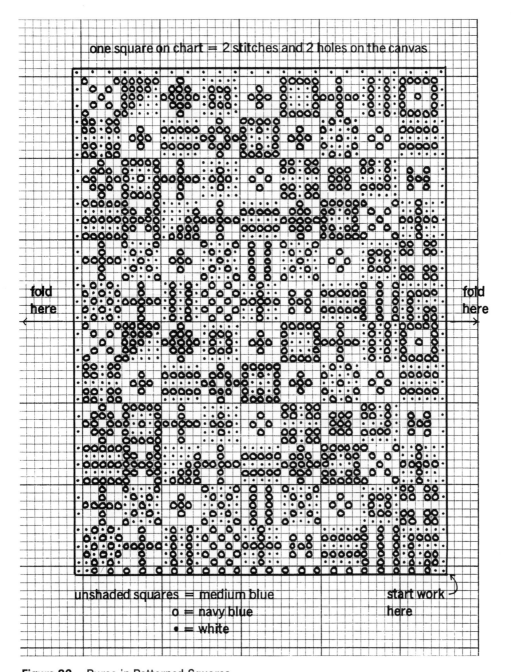

Figure 82   Purse in Patterned Squares

123

squares within squares ✱✱
(Plate 7)

Each square patch is framed with a border in a plain color. When all the patches are assembled, another border is added around the outside, consistent with the orderly appearance of this design.

FINISHED SIZE   Approx. 16 by 16 inches

you need

▶ Persian needlepoint wool in 10-yard skeins:

Copper	6	(60 yards)
Orange	4	(40 yards)
Light orange	4	(40 yards)
Beige	2	(20 yards)
Cream	4	(40 yards)

▶ A piece of ten-mesh-to-one-inch mono canvas measuring 20 x 20 inches

▶ A number 18 tapestry needle

METHOD

1. The entire design is worked over four mesh of the canvas.
2. Find the center of the canvas as shown in Chapter 2.
3. Find the center square of the chart as shown in Chapter 2.
4. Begin working at center square, following chart shown in Figure 83, and sewing from right to left, toward left edge. Return to center square and complete center row to right edge. Continue working in rows until entire chart is completed.

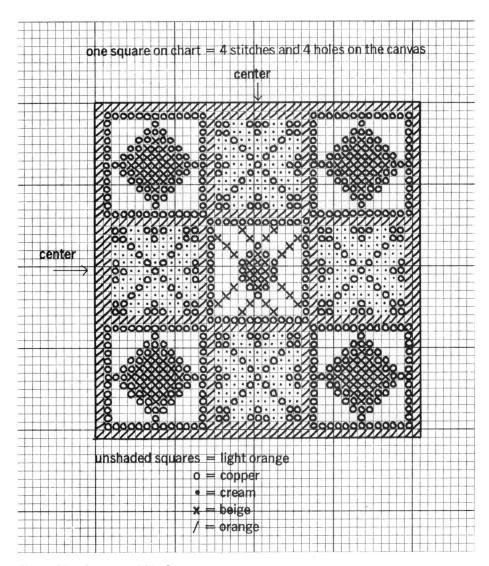

one square on chart = 4 stitches and 4 holes on the canvas

center

center

unshaded squares = light orange
o = copper
• = cream
x = beige
/ = orange

Figure 83 Squares within Squares

american indian designs

The first five designs in this chapter belong together in a group. I mounted the five completed panels on board to display in a cluster on the wall. This is the reason for the same colors being used for each design. You can, of course, make any number of these pictures, from one to five, and alter the color schemes to suit your own needs and taste. The figurative motifs represent some of the most frequently recurring decorative themes in South American Indian crafts, and I thought that it would add impact to the designs if the five were displayed together.

If you do decide to make all five panels, you will need to make some reduction in the quantities of yarn specified. Chapter 2 gives some helpful advice on how to calculate your requirements. The panels are so simple that I can wholeheartedly recommend them to the beginner.

Aztec Bird Panel

aztec bird panel *

FINISHED SIZE   Approx. 10½ x 17½ inches

you need

‣ Persian needlepoint wool in 10-yard skeins:

Bright gold	9	(90 yards)
Black	2	(20 yards)
Copper	4	(40 yards)

‣ A piece of ten-mesh-to-one-inch mono canvas measuring 14 x 21 inches
‣ A number 18 tapestry needle

METHOD

1. The entire design is worked over four mesh of the canvas.
2. Start in lower right corner, at a point 2 inches up from bottom and in from side edge.
3. Following the chart shown in Figure 84, begin work where indicated by the arrow. Work in rows across, until entire chart is completed.

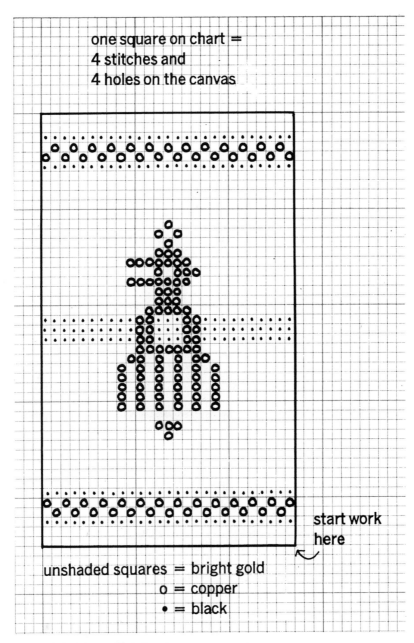

one square on chart =
4 stitches and
4 holes on the canvas

start work here

unshaded squares = bright gold
o = copper
• = black

Figure 84   Aztec Bird Panel

Colombian Armed Figure

colombian armed figure *

FINISHED SIZE   Approx 10½ x 17½ inches

you need

▶ Persian needlepoint wool in 10-yard skeins:

Bright gold	7	(70 yards)
Cream	3	(30 yards)
Copper	3	(30 yards)
Black	1	(10 yards)

▶ A piece of ten-mesh-to-one-inch mono canvas measuring 14 x 21 inches

▶ A number 18 tapestry needle

METHOD

1. The entire design is worked over four mesh of the canvas.
2. Start in lower right corner, at a point 2 inches up from bottom and in from side edge.
3. Following the chart shown in Figure 85, begin work where indicated by the arrow. Work in rows across, until entire chart is completed.

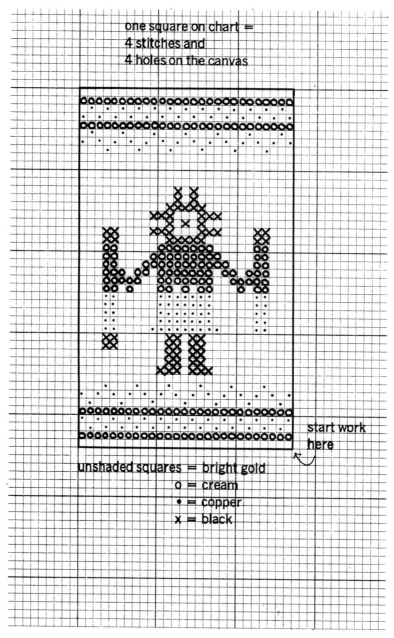

Figure 85 Colombian Armed Figure

head of a god *
(Plate 8)

FINISHED SIZE   Approx. 10½ x 17½ inches

you need

▶ Persian needlepoint wool in 10-yard skeins:

Bright gold	8	(80 yards)
Black	3	(30 yards)
Copper	3	(30 yards)

▶ A piece of ten-mesh-to-one-inch mono canvas measuring 14 x 21 inches

▶ A number 18 tapestry needle

METHOD

1. The entire design is worked over four mesh of the canvas.
2. Start in lower right corner, at a point 2 inches up from bottom and in from side edge.
3. Following the chart shown in Figure 86, begin work where indicated by the arrow. Work in rows across, until entire chart is completed.

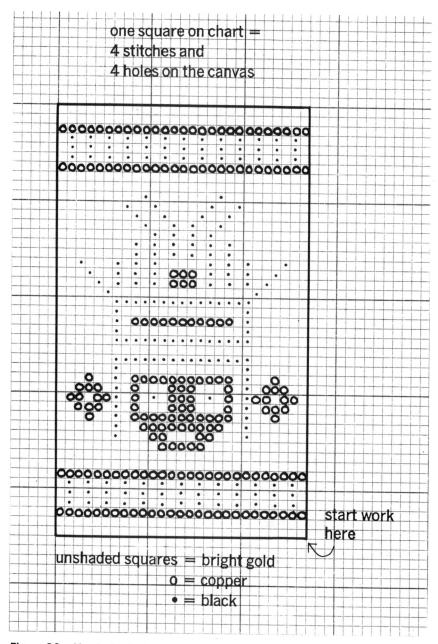

one square on chart =
4 stitches and
4 holes on the canvas

start work
here

unshaded squares = bright gold
o = copper
• = black

Figure 86 Head of a God

aztec eagle *

FINISHED SIZE   Approx. 10½ x 17½ inches

you need

▶ Persian needlepoint wool in 10-yard skeins:

Bright gold	7	(70 yards)
Cream	3	(30 yards)
Copper	4	(40 yards)
Black	1	(10 yards)

▶ A piece of ten-mesh-to-one-inch mono canvas measuring 14 x 21 inches

▶ A number 18 tapestry needle

METHOD

1. The entire design is worked over four mesh of the canvas.
2. Start in lower right corner, at a point 2 inches up from bottom and in from side edge.
3. Following the chart shown in Figure 87, begin work where indicated by the arrow. Work in rows across, until entire chart is completed.

Aztec Eagle

136

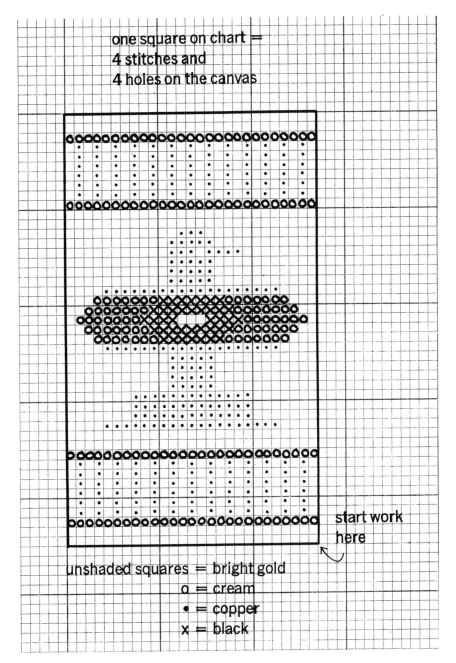

Figure 87 Aztec Eagle

137

figure of a god *

FINISHED SIZE   Approx. 10½ x 17½ inches

you need

▸ Persian needlepoint wool in 10-yard skeins:

Bright gold	7	(70 yards)
Copper	3	(30 yards)
Black	4	(40 yards)

▸ A piece of ten-mesh-to-one-inch mono canvas measuring 14 x 21 inches
▸ A number 18 tapestry needle

METHOD

1. The entire design is worked over four mesh of the canvas.
2. Start in lower right corner, at a point 2 inches up from bottom and in from side edge.
3. Following the chart shown in Figure 88, begin work where indicated by the arrow. Work in rows across, until entire chart is completed.

Figure of a God

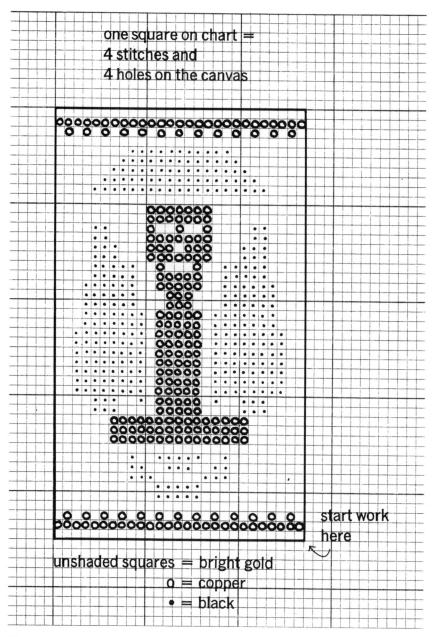

Figure 88   Figure of a God

purse in basket weave **

The patterning and coloring for this design were taken directly from a North American Indian basket. The rectangle of canvas, when completed, folds at the center to make a small bag with a zippered top. Instructions for finishing the bag are given in Chapter 3.

FINISHED SIZE   Approx. 9½ x 12½ inches (9½ x 6 inches when folded)

you need

▶ Persian needlepoint wool in 10-yard skeins:

Chocolate	6	(60 yards)
Medium brown	2	(20 yards)
Winter white	3	(30 yards)
Light brown	2	(20 yards)

▶ A piece of ten-mesh-to-one-inch mono canvas measuring 12 x 14 inches

▶ A number 18 tapestry needle

METHOD

1. The entire design is worked over two mesh of the canvas.
2. Start in lower right corner, at a point 1 inch up from bottom and in from side edge.
3. Following the chart shown in Figure 89, begin work where indicated by the arrow. Work in rows across, until entire chart is completed.

Purse in Basket Weave

one square on chart = 2 stitches and 2 holes on the canvas

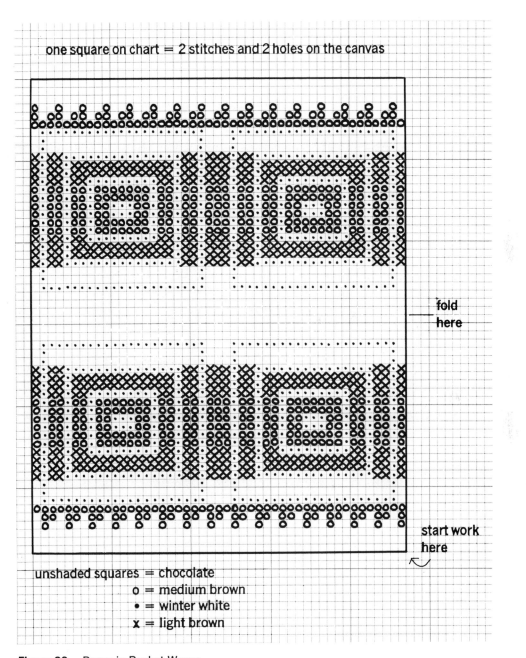

fold
here

start work
here

unshaded squares = chocolate
    o = medium brown
    • = winter white
    x = light brown

Figure 89   Purse in Basket Weave

beaded eyeglasses case ✳✳✳

Based on a North American Indian beaded fringe, the eyeglasses case is worked in one continuous strip, then folded across the center, as shown on the chart. For full instructions on how to finish the case, please turn to Chapter 3.

FINISHED SIZE   Approx. 14 x 3 inches (7 x 3 inches when folded)

you need

▶ Persian needlepoint wool in 10-yard skeins:

Winter white	3	(30 yards)
Brown	3	(30 yards)

▶ A piece of eighteen-mesh-to-one-inch mono canvas measuring 16 x 5 inches

▶ A number 22 tapestry needle

SPECIAL NOTE   The entire design is worked with only *two* strands of the Persian yarn instead of the usual three.

METHOD

1. The entire design is worked over four mesh of the canvas.
2. Start in lower right corner, at a point 1 inch up from bottom and in from side edge.
3. Following the chart shown in Figure 90, begin work where indicated by the arrow. Work in rows across, until entire chart is completed.

Beaded Eyeglasses Case

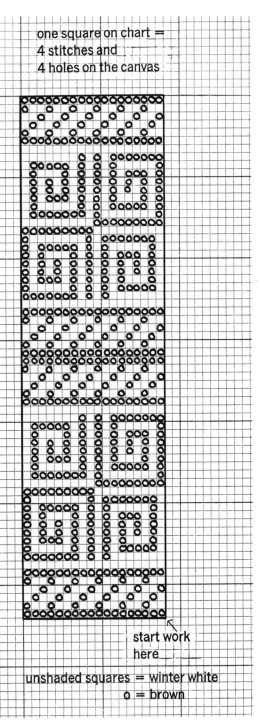

one square on chart =
4 stitches and
4 holes on the canvas

start work
here

unshaded squares = winter white
o = brown

Figure 90   Beaded Eyeglasses Case

145

aztec wall hanging ***
(Plate 9)

The faces, figures, birds, and borders used in this panel can be found on any number of South American Indian pots, textiles, and other artifacts. Although the design has been given the most difficult three-star rating, it is not complicated to sew. The high rating results mainly from the width of the panel, which makes the canvas awkward to handle, except for those who have gained considerable sewing expertise. Turn to Chapter 3 for ways to mount a hanging like this one.

FINISHED SIZE   Approx. 26½ x 27¼ inches

you need

▸ Persian needlepoint wool in 10-yard skeins:

Winter white	41	(410 yards)
Brown	5	(50 yards)
Coffee	5	(50 yards)
Red	4	(40 yards)
Copper	5	(50 yards)

▸ A piece of ten-mesh-to-one-inch mono canvas measuring 30 x 31 inches

▸ A number 18 tapestry needle

METHOD

1. The entire design is worked over four mesh of the canvas.
2. Start in lower right corner, at a point 2 inches up from bottom and in from side edge.
3. Following the chart shown in Figure 91, begin work where indicated by the arrow. Work in rows across, until entire chart is completed.

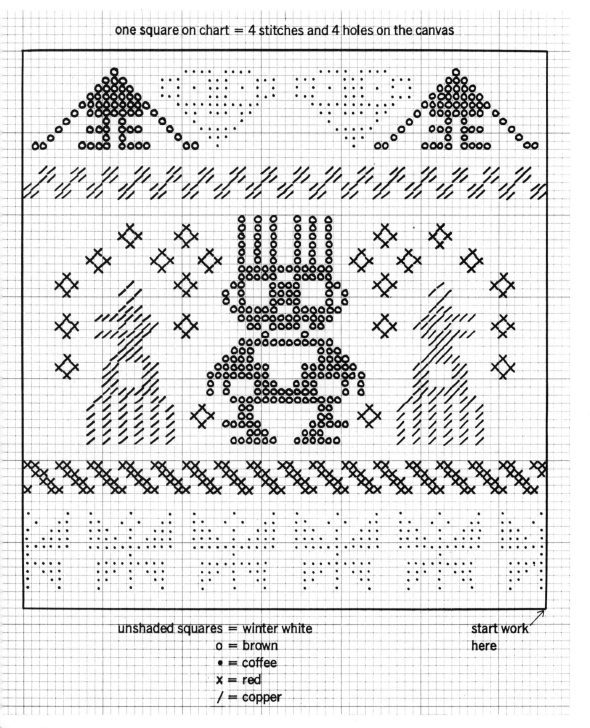

one square on chart = 4 stitches and 4 holes on the canvas

unshaded squares = winter white

o = brown

• = coffee

x = red

/ = copper

start work here

Figure 91 Aztec Wall Hanging

147

indian fabric square ✱✱✱
(Plate 10)

This design is based on a richly appliquéd North American Indian fabric. The layout of the pattern and the color combinations have been kept as close as possible to the original cloth. Should you wish to extend the design in any direction, it would be simple to accomplish, provided that you chart out your alterations before sewing and allow extra yarn in proportion to the enlargement.

This particular pattern would look effective if alternated with plain squares in brilliant colors to make a wall hanging. The method for doing this is described in Chapter 2 and illustrated in Figure 28.

The design is marked "difficult" because of the insertion of two rows of Bargello stitches in the pattern. Apart from this factor, nothing could be simpler to make than these bands of brilliant color.

FINISHED SIZE   Approx. 16 x 16 inches

you need

▶ Persian needlepoint wool in 10-yard skeins:

White	6	(60 yards)
Red	5	(50 yards)
Orange	3	(30 yards)
Navy blue	6	(60 yards)
Yellow	1	(10 yards)
Light green	1	(10 yards)

▶ A piece of ten-mesh-to-one-inch mono canvas measuring 20 x 20 inches

▶ A number 18 tapestry needle

SPECIAL NOTE   A row of Bargello stitches is worked over two squares of the chart at the top and in the lower half of the canvas. A subsidiary chart for working these zig-zag stitches is given in Figure 92.

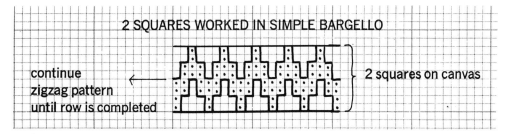

Figure 92   Zigzag Bargello Inset

METHOD

1. The entire design is worked over four mesh of the canvas.
2. Start in lower right corner, at a point 2 inches up from bottom and in from side edge.
3. Following the chart shown in Figure 93, begin work where indicated by the arrow. Work in rows across, until entire chart is completed.

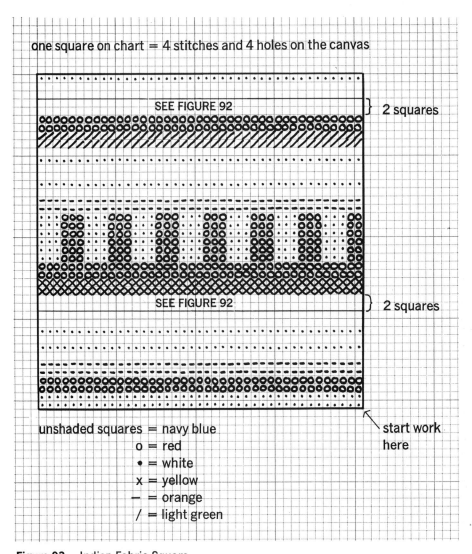

one square on chart = 4 stitches and 4 holes on the canvas

SEE FIGURE 92 } 2 squares

SEE FIGURE 92 } 2 squares

unshaded squares = navy blue
o = red
• = white
x = yellow
— = orange
/ = light green

start work here

Figure 93 Indian Fabric Square

150

african designs

A predominance of black and white, with brilliant colors, and geometric motifs typify the woven textiles of West Africa, which I have used as a source for the designs in this chapter. I have followed the traditional colors and arrangements of motifs as closely as possible. However, if you see a pattern that you like, but are unable to use any of the bright colors in your home, you should feel free to make changes to suit your own decorating requirements. If you want the look of authenticity as an added bonus to your canvas work, then I suggest you copy the colors I have taken directly from the fabrics.

African textiles are often woven on a small hand loom, producing a fabric of not more than a few inches wide. The strips produced in this way are subsequently sewn together by hand to create a larger area of fabric. In the same way, you can use the African squares to create wall hangings and rugs as described in Chapter 2. Sewing small sections together to make larger items seems particularly appropriate in working an African design, where such a process is part of a real and living tradition.

To add extra decoration to your canvases, try attaching tassels made in bright colors to the finished piece, not just in corners but all over the design. You can also apply embroidery stitches to the surface of the straight-stitch canvas, wherever you feel they would add color and interest to the design, and most especially over the joins of a squared rug or wall hanging. Let your imagination respond to the beautiful colors and textures of these patterns.

mosaic tcharka ✤
(Plate 11)

FINISHED SIZE   Approx. 16 x 16 inches

you need

▶ Persian needlepoint wool in 10-yard skeins:

White	6	(60 yards)
Red	4	(40 yards)
Black	6	(60 yards)
Turquoise	2	(20 yards)
Orange	4	(40 yards)

▶ A piece of ten-mesh-to-one-inch mono canvas measuring 20 x 20 inches

▶ A number 18 tapestry needle

METHOD

1. The entire design is worked over four mesh of the canvas.
2. Start in lower right corner, at a point 2 inches up from bottom and in from side edge.
3. Following the chart shown in Figure 94, begin work where indicated by the arrow. Work in rows across, until entire chart is completed.

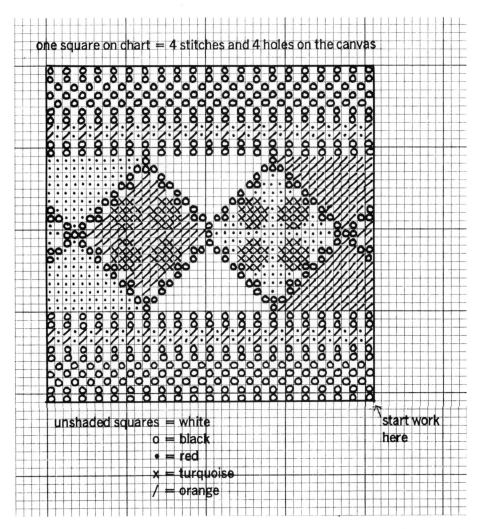

one square on chart = 4 stitches and 4 holes on the canvas

unshaded squares = white
o = black
• = red
x = turquoise
/ = orange

start work here

Figure 94 Mosaic Tcharka

panel from niger **

FINISHED SIZE   Approx. 22 x 20 inches

you need

▶ Persian needlepoint wool in 10-yard skeins:

Black	12	(120 yards)
White	6	(60 yards)
Orange	3	(30 yards)
Turquoise	1	(10 yards)
Red	1	(10 yards)

▶ A piece of ten-mesh-to-one-inch mono canvas measuring 26 x 24 inches

▶ A number 18 tapestry needle

METHOD

1. The entire design is worked over four mesh of the canvas.
2. Start in lower right corner, at a point 2 inches up from bottom and in from side edge.
3. Following the chart shown in Figure 95, begin work where indicated by the arrow. Work in rows across, until entire chart is completed.

Panel from Niger

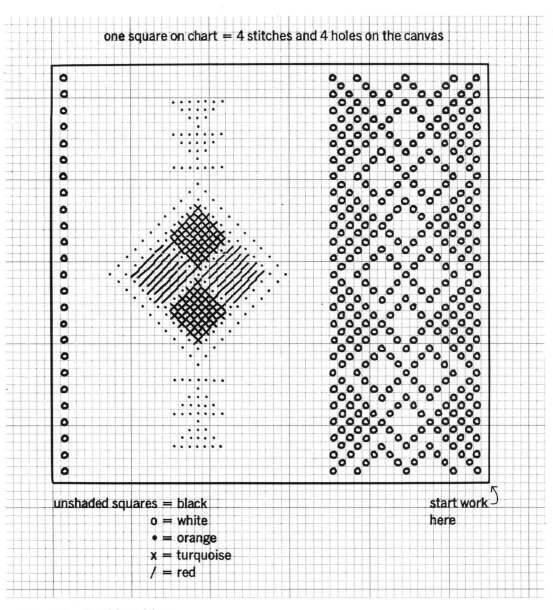

one square on chart = 4 stitches and 4 holes on the canvas

unshaded squares = black
o = white
• = orange
x = turquoise
/ = red

start work here

Figure 95 Panel from Niger

156

african wall hanging in strips ✳✳✳
(Plate 12)

For instructions on how to mount the canvas for hanging, please turn to Chapter 3.

FINISHED SIZE   Approx. 26 x 30½ inches

you need

▶ Persian needlepoint wool in 10-yard skeins:

White	28	(280 yards)
Black	23	(230 yards)
Red	4	(40 yards)
Orange	2	(20 yards)
Turquoise	2	(20 yards)

▶ A piece of ten-mesh-to-one-inch mono canvas measuring 30 x 35 inches

▶ A number 18 tapestry needle

METHOD

1. The entire design is worked over four mesh of the canvas.
2. Start in lower right corner, at a point 2 inches up from bottom and in from side edge.
3. Following the chart shown in Figure 96, begin work where indicated by the arrow. Work in rows across, until entire chart is completed.

Figure 96 African Wall Hanging in Strips

african wall hanging in diamonds ✲✲✲
(Plate 13)

For instructions on how to mount the canvas for hanging, please turn to Chapter 3.

FINISHED SIZE   Approx. 23½ x 23½ inches

you need

▶ Persian needlepoint wool in 10-yard skeins:

White	19	(190 yards)
Black	17	(170 yards)
Red	5	(50 yards)
Bottle green	2	(20 yards)
Orange	1	(10 yards)

▶ A piece of ten-mesh-to-one-inch mono canvas measuring 28 x 28 inches

▶ A number 18 tapestry needle

METHOD

1. The entire design is worked over two mesh of the canvas.
2. Start in lower right corner, at a point 2 inches up from bottom and in from side edge.
3. Following the chart shown in Figure 97, begin work indicated by the arrow. Work in rows across, until entire chart is completed.

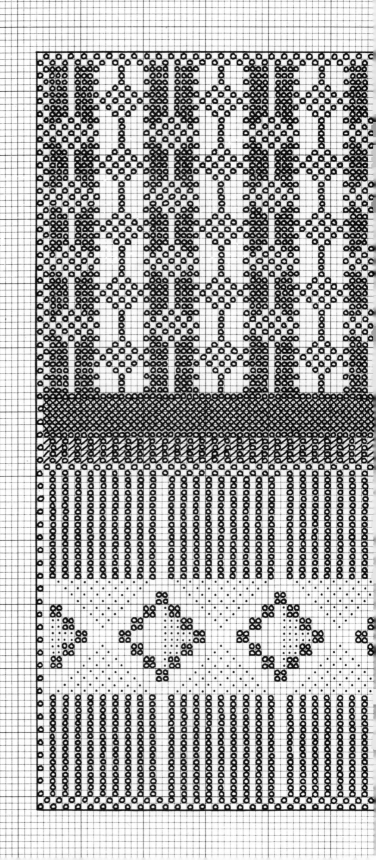

Figure 97
African Wall Hanging
in Diamonds

161

document folder in african strips ✸✸

The finished canvas is folded in two places, as shown in the chart, to make an overlapping flap. Full finishing instructions appear in Chapter 3.

FINISHED SIZE   Approx. 16 x 28 inches (16 x 12 inches when folded)

you need

▶ Persian needlepoint wool in 10-yard skeins:

White	11	(110 yards)
Black	12	(120 yards)
Red	5	(50 yards)
Orange	5	(50 yards)

▶ A piece of ten-mesh-to-one-inch mono canvas measuring 20 x 32 inches
▶ A number 18 tapestry needle

METHOD

1. The entire design is worked over four mesh of the canvas.
2. Start in lower right corner, at a point 2 inches up from bottom and in from side edge.
3. Following the chart shown in Figure 98, begin work where indicated by the arrow. Work in rows across, until entire chart is completed.

Document Folder in African Strips

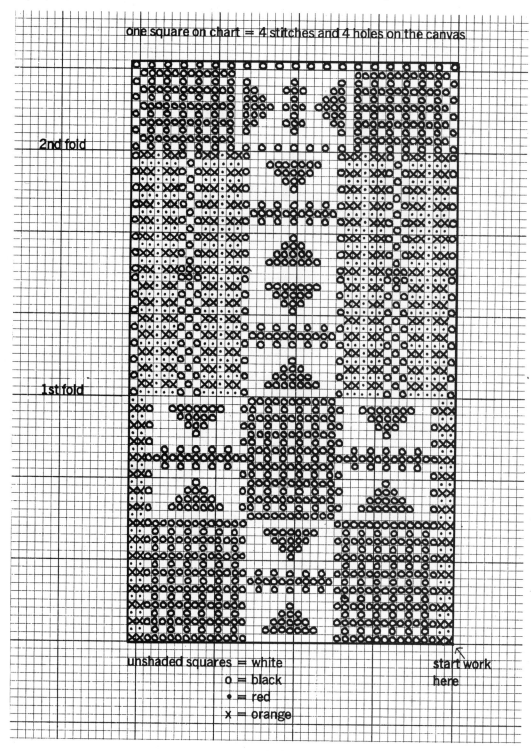

one square on chart = 4 stitches and 4 holes on the canvas

2nd fold

1st fold

unshaded squares = white
o = black
• = red
x = orange

start work here

Figure 98   Document Folder in African Strips

egyptian designs

The familiar symbols of Egyptian art, such as the scarab beetle, the eye of the god Ra, and the colorful hieroglyphic writing are represented in these designs. I have also included some rich mosaic patterns, taken from friezes and wall paintings, to add some abstract designs to the stylized figurative pieces. The colorings have been kept as close as possible to the originals but can be changed to suit your own taste or room setting.

Hieroglyphic Panel

hieroglyphic panel *

FINISHED SIZE   Approx. 10½ x 17½ inches

you need

▶ Persian needlepoint wool in 10-yard skeins:

Beige	10	(100 yards)
Dark brown	5	(50 yards)
Light brown	2	(20 yards)

▶ A piece of ten-mesh-to-one-inch mono canvas measuring 14 x 21 inches

▶ A number 18 tapestry needle

METHOD

1. The entire design is worked over four mesh of the canvas.
2. Start in lower right corner, at a point 2 inches up from bottom and in from side edge.
3. Following the chart shown in Figure 99, begin work where indicated by the arrow. Work in rows across, until entire chart is completed.

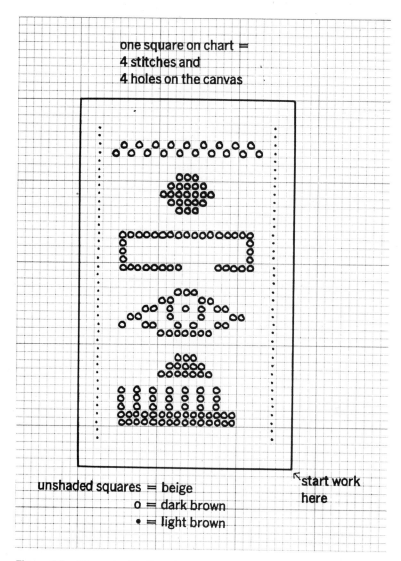

one square on chart =
4 stitches and
4 holes on the canvas

unshaded squares = beige
o = dark brown
• = light brown

start work here

Figure 99 Hieroglyphic Panel

scarab beetle *

FINISHED SIZE   Approx. 16 x 16 inches

you need

▶ Persian needlepoint wool in 10-yard skeins:

Black	3	(30 yards)
White	10	(100 yards)
Orange	3	(30 yards)
Dark turquoise	7	(70 yards)
Light turquoise	2	(20 yards)

▶ A piece of ten-mesh-to-one-inch mono canvas measuring 20 x 20 inches

▶ A number 18 tapestry needle

METHOD

1. The entire design is worked over four mesh of the canvas.
2. Start in lower right corner, at a point 2 inches up from bottom and in from side edge.
3. Following the chart shown in Figure 100, begin work where indicated by the arrow. Work in rows across, until entire chart is completed.

Scarab Beetle

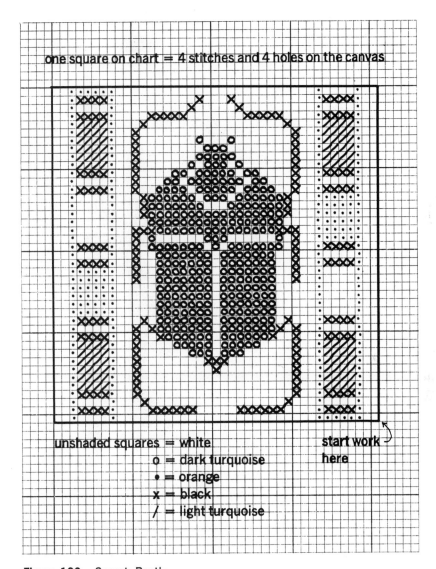

one square on chart = 4 stitches and 4 holes on the canvas

unshaded squares = white
o = dark turquoise
• = orange
x = black
/ = light turquoise

start work here

Figure 100 Scarab Beetle

171

eye of ra *
(Plate 14)

FINISHED SIZE   Approx. 14 x 14 inches

you need

▶ Persian needlepoint wool in 10-yard skeins:

White	8	(80 yards)
Black	3	(30 yards)
Turquoise	1	(10 yards)
Orange	3	(30 yards)

▶ A piece of ten-mesh-to-one-inch mono canvas measuring 18 x 18 inches

▶ A number 18 tapestry needle

METHOD

1. The entire design is worked over four mesh of the canvas.
2. Start in lower right corner, at a point 2 inches up from bottom and in from side edge.
3. Following the chart shown in Figure 101, begin work where indicated by the arrow. Work in rows across, until entire chart is completed.

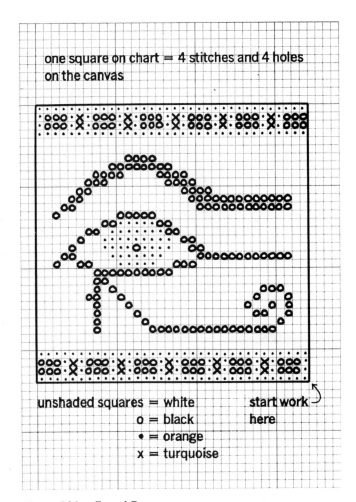

one square on chart = 4 stitches and 4 holes on the canvas

unshaded squares = white
o = black
• = orange
x = turquoise

start work here

Figure 101   Eye of Ra

egyptian mosaic **
(Plate 15)

FINISHED SIZE   Approx. 14 x 14 inches

you need

▶ Persian needlepoint wool in 10-yard skeins:

Aubergine	4	(40 yards)
Royal blue	5	(50 yards)
Gold	6	(60 yards)
Red	6	(60 yards)
Turquoise	6	(60 yards)

▶ A piece of ten-mesh-to-one-inch mono canvas measuring 18 x 18 inches

▶ A number 18 tapestry needle

METHOD

1. The entire design is worked over two mesh of the canvas.
2. Start in lower right corner, at a point 2 inches up from bottom and in from side edge.
3. Following the chart shown in Figure 102, begin work where indicated by the arrow. Work in rows across, until entire chart is completed.

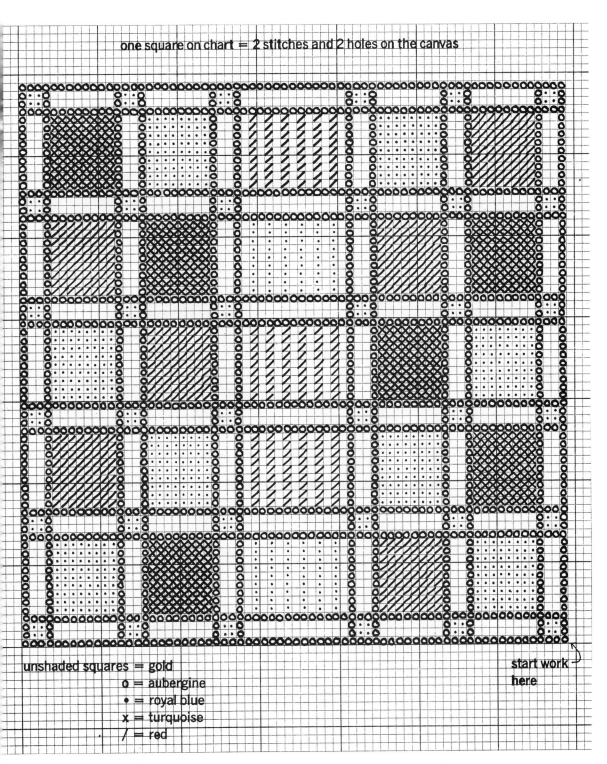

one square on chart = 2 stitches and 2 holes on the canvas

unshaded squares = gold
ο = aubergine
• = royal blue
x = turquoise
/ = red

start work here

Figure 102 Egyptian Mosaic

175

egyptian hieroglyphics **
(Plate 16)

FINISHED SIZE   Approx. 14 x 14 inches

you need

▸ Persian needlepoint wool in 10-yard skeins:

Gold	10	(100 yards)
Black	4	(40 yards)
Copper	2	(20 yards)

▸ A piece of ten-mesh-to-one-inch mono canvas measuring 18 x 18 inches

▸ A number 18 tapestry needle

METHOD

1. The entire design is worked over two mesh of the canvas.
2. Start in lower right corner, at a point 2 inches up from bottom and in from side edge.
3. Following the chart shown in Figure 103, begin work where indicated by the arrow. Work in rows across, until entire chart is completed.

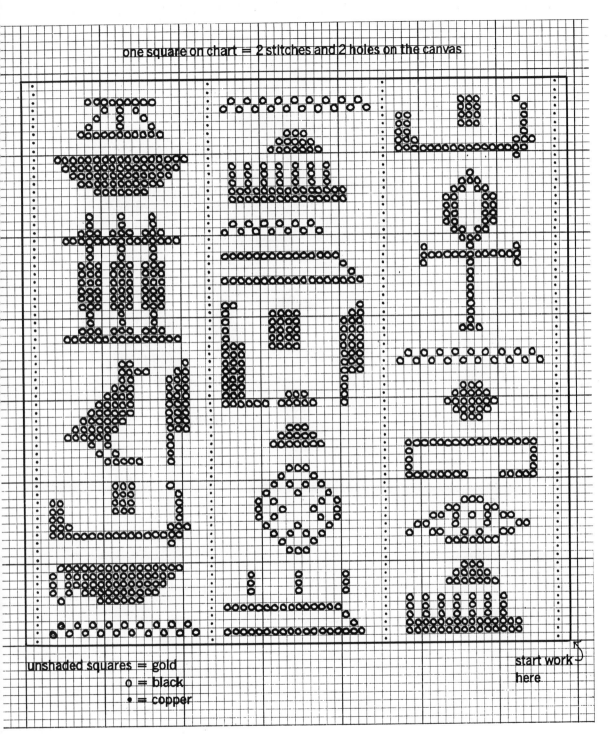

Figure 103 Egyptian Hieroglyphics

177

ankh eyeglasses case ✳✳✳

The eyeglasses case is worked in one continuous strip and then folded across the center, as shown on the chart. The ankh appears upside down on one half of the design, so that it will, in fact, be the correct way up after the canvas is folded. For full instructions on how to finish the case, please turn to Chapter 3.

FINISHED SIZE   Approx. 14 x 4 inches (7 x 4 inches when folded)

you need

▶ Persian needlepoint wool in 10-yard skeins:

Gold	4	(40 yards)
Copper	1	(10 yards)

▶ A piece of ten-mesh-to-one-inch mono canvas measuring 16 x 6 inches

▶ A number 22 tapestry needle

SPECIAL NOTE   The entire design is worked with only *two* strands of the Persian yarn instead of the usual three.

METHOD

1. The entire design is worked over four mesh of the canvas.
2. Start in lower right corner, at a point 1 inch up from bottom and in from side edge.
3. Following the chart shown in Figure 104, begin work where indicated by the arrow. Work in rows across, until entire chart is completed.

Ankh Eyeglasses Case

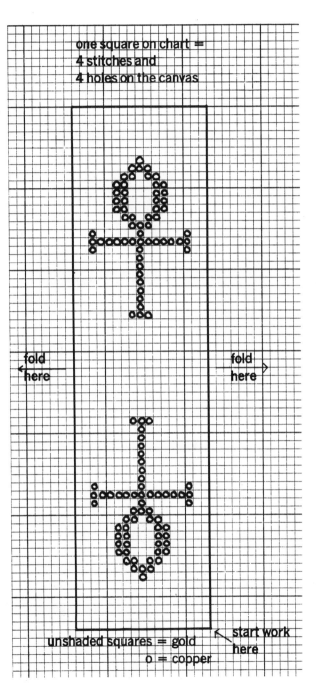

one square on chart =
4 stitches and
4 holes on the canvas

fold
here

fold
here

start work
here

unshaded squares = gold

o = copper

Figure 104   Ankh Eyeglasses Case

179

Purse in Eye-of-Ra Motif

purse in eye-of-ra motif ✳✳✳

This small purse could be made into an eyeglasses case or a cosmetics bag. A selection of methods for finishing rectangular shapes like this is given in Chapter 3.

FINISHED SIZE   Approx. 7 x 8 inches (7 x 4 inches when folded)

you need

▶ Persian needlepoint wool in 10-yard skeins:

Gold	4	(40 yards)
Copper	2	(20 yards)

▶ A piece of eighteen-mesh-to-one-inch mono canvas measuring 9 x 10 inches

▶ A number 22 tapestry needle

SPECIAL NOTE   The entire design is worked with only two strands of the Persian yarn instead of the usual three.

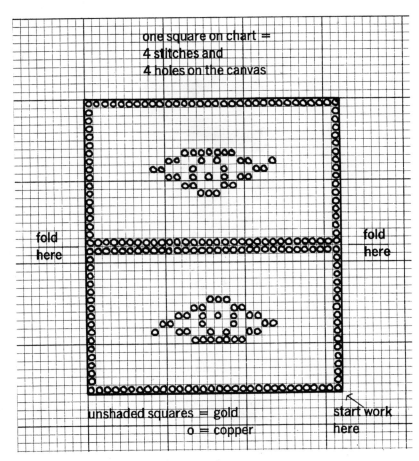

Figure 105   Purse in Eye-of-Ra Motif

METHOD

1. The entire design is worked over four mesh of the canvas.
2. Start in lower right corner, at a point 1 inch up from bottom and in from side edge.
3. Following the chart shown in Figure 105, begin work where indicated by the arrow. Work in rows across, until entire chart is completed.

mosaic frieze *

FINISHED SIZE   Approx. 14 x 14 inches

you need

▶ Persian needlepoint wool in 10-yard skeins:

Black	7	(70 yards)
Dark gold	5	(50 yards)
Medium gold	3	(30 yards)
Light gold	4	(40 yards)

▶ A piece of ten-mesh-to-one-inch mono canvas measuring 18 x 18 inches

▶ A number 18 tapestry needle

METHOD

1. The entire design is worked over four mesh of the canvas.
2. Start in lower right corner, at a point 2 inches up from bottom and in from side edge.
3. Following the chart shown in Figure 106, begin work where indicated by the arrow. Work in rows across, until entire chart is completed.

Mosaic Frieze

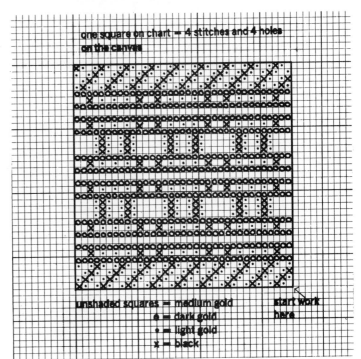

Figure 106 Mosaic Frieze

one square on chart = 4 stitches and 4 holes on the canvas

unshaded squares = medium gold
o = dark gold
• = light gold
x = black

start work here

eyeglasses case in hieroglyphics ✿✿✿

This case is worked in the same way as the Ankh Eyeglasses Case. Please read the note at the beginning of that project.

FINISHED SIZE   Approx. 13½ x 4 inches (6¾ x 4 inches folded)

you need

▶ Persian needlepoint wool in 10-yard skeins:

| Light brown | 3 | (30 yards) |
| Medium brown | 2 | (20 yards) |

▶ A piece of eighteen-mesh-to-one-inch mono canvas measuring 16 x 6 inches
▶ A number 22 tapestry needle

SPECIAL NOTE   The entire design is worked with only *two* strands of the Persian yarn instead of the usual three.

METHOD

1. The entire design is worked over four mesh of the canvas.
2. Start in lower right corner, at a point 1 inch up from bottom and in from side edge.
3. Following the chart shown in Figure 107, begin work where indicated by the arrow. Work in rows across, until entire chart is completed.

Eyeglasses Case in Hieroglyphics

one square on chart =
4 stitches and
4 holes on the canvas

fold
here ←

→ fold
here

↖ start work
here

unshaded squares = light brown

o = medium brown

Figure 107 Eyeglasses Case in Hieroglyphics

185